HACK THE COLLEGE ESSAY
PARENT GUIDE

HACK THE COLLEGE ESSAY
PARENT GUIDE

John Dewis

From the author of
HACK THE COLLEGE ESSAY

Hack the College Essay
Hackthecollegeessay.com

ISBN-13: 978-0-578-35558-0

Cover: Harvard House, Cambridge, Mass.
Printed in the United States of America

JOHNDEWIS@YAHOO.COM

For my mother – who tells the truth as if it were made up

If I knew for a certainty that a man was coming to my house with the conscious design of doing me good, I should run for my life.

THOREAU

Although wisdom is common to all, most live as if it were their own.

HERACLITUS

Every single thing, to the extent that it exists, must persist in the way that it is.

SPINOZA

Because the boogie-woogie is in him, and it has got to get out.

JOHNNIE LEE HOOKER

Table of Contents

x

"How-tos" by chapter

Chapter 1: Gamer
How to say yes
How to ask the right questions

Chapter 2: The Demonstration Trap
How to think not show
How to call bullshit

Chapter 3: Bitcoin Miner
How to be uncomfortable
How to extract feelings from facts

Chapter 4: How it Sounds if You (the Parent) Write it
How not to micromanage the essay
How not to macro-manage the essay

Chapter 5: How it Sounds if the Counselor Writes it
How not to translate the essay into an essay
How to be all things to one person

Chapter 6: How it Sounds if Your Kid Writes it
How to stalk an elephant
How to play Devil's Advocate and lose

Chapter 7: The Opposite of Boring
How to listen
How to let it be confusing enough

Chapter 8: The Opposite of Lonely
How to write two essays at once
How to write the essay in one hour

Chapter 9: The Opposite of Writing
How to think on paper
How to fix the headlight on a Pontiac Fiero

Preface

Dear Parents,

This book is advice, but it's also about advice. It's about the advice you give your kids when they're trying to write their college essays.

I think it's lucky if your kid has a parent like you who wants to help. It means your kid has a parent who cares. My goal here is for your help to be lucky for another reason: that it helps your kid get in.

I believe helping can be better than not helping, and there are ways for you to help that are practical, ethical, and fun. I also have reason to believe most help on the college essay is none of those things. I'd like to help your help actually help.

I wrote *Hack the College Essay* for kids who feel lost with the essay and don't have access to tutors. This leaves out another group of people who might feel lost and don't have tutors: parents!

The *Parent Guide* is for you. I hope you like it.

John Dewis
South Pasadena, CA
January 1, 2022

Introduction – License to help

I remember spending a day painting in a field with a friend. We were far from civilization, looking at some trees. We had our easels and canvases and were doing our best with oils to capture the trees. We were eighteen and in a painting class at Deep Springs College.

My friend's father was a great business success and was visiting from New York. He walked out into the field to watch us paint. He walked up next to his son and said, "Hey, I like how you're doing those trees."

"Thanks, Dad."

"But you shouldn't be afraid to paint them boldly." My friend put a little more muscle into it. "Yes, that's it, but look how yellow that tree is in the light."

"I see it."

"Yes, but here, look, you can really go for it. Make your mark, otherwise it's just paint." He held his son's hand on the brush. "No, more like this."

My friend let go of the brush and his father jabbed bright yellow paint on the canvas. He looked at the tree and jabbed some more. My friend stepped away from the painting and walked back across the field. This became the day I spent in a field painting next to my friend's father.

This is not an anecdote about plagiarism. My friend would never have passed his father's painting off as his own. It's about the perils of helping your kid. It's about the road paved with good intentions, and about the things we can't see even when they're right in front of us.

One common piece of advice on the college essay appears no-nonsense: *Just step away*. It also has moral appeal. It might feel like the antidote to helicopter parenting.

> *This is really her job and the best thing I can do is stay out of it.*
> *I need to remember that this has nothing to do with me.*
> *It's a rite of passage and she's just going to have to figure it out.*

I think these sentiments warrant revisiting for three practical reasons:

1) Helping your kid is also moral
2) Most parents want to help their kids
3) Most parents end up helping anyway

Your help is better if you don't feel conflicted about it. You can be both confident in your role and cautious in your contributions. Let's look more closely at the three reasons, lest you find yourself standing alone in a field holding a paintbrush.

1) Helping your kid is also moral

Our job as parents includes both guiding our kids and letting them make errors. It's not obvious to me that the college essay is the place to let them err.

One reason is that getting in, having choices, or earning a scholarship might matter. There is also a subtler reason: Left to her own devices, your kid is unlikely to write an honest essay! If we hope to raise honest kids, your participation has a moral advantage.

Students are not deliberately lying or misleading admissions. They are buying into a way of thinking that makes them generic when they think they are being deep.

Replacing themselves with a genre of kid is deceptive, and so is replacing actual experience with a genre of experience.

In short, they are pretending not to be who they are.

In *Hack the College Essay* I explain why this is a failing strategy. It robs your kid of the one best strategy she has: to write the essay no one else could. I also explain how this phenomenon arises and how she can spot it and do better. In *Hack the College Essay Parent Guide* I show you how to spot it and help your kid do better.

A paradox: does speaking for oneself require a push from someone else? Sometimes the push is just permission. I think you're doing a good thing if you help your kid speak for herself. It's a goal of education, and many high schools are failing to reach it. As a parent, how do you help cultivate the skill rather than cover up its absence?

Your help is not to write the essay. It is not the thinking, reflecting, analyzing, realizing, concluding, shaping, or wordsmithing. I hope this comes as a relief.

But what's left? The stuff that makes those other things possible. It's listening, prompting, questioning, prodding, remembering, wondering, and extracting. Simply put, the job of helping is not to *do* the work but to *elicit* the work.

2) Most parents want to help their kids

Many parents struggle to reconcile the impulse to help with the warning against it. Let's trust the impulse and then make sure it improves the essay.

A lot of the advice in this book is about how to have a conversation with your kid that helps her write a great essay. A conversation is collaborative, by definition, even if the essay itself is not.

If you keep that distinction clear, it can free you from worrying about whether you are helping too much or not enough. Good conversation is fun and there are no rules against it.

3) Most parents end up helping anyway

Sadly, most help hurts the essay. Even careful, well-meaning help:

I'll edit your final draft for grammar
I'll make sure you weren't shy about putting your best foot forward
I'll see that you didn't forget to show what a kind person you are

These last-minute adjustments might seem the least disruptive, but they are often responsible for the worst adulterations of student work. Parents edit out idiosyncratic details and edit in impressive lessons.

What's wrong with that? I show in *Hack the College Essay* why most lessons do not help admissions get to know anyone. Lessons belong to everyone because it's the nature of lessons to be universal.

The actual details of our lives and thoughts, however, belong only to us because no one else in the universe did the same thing at the same time in the same way. If you let your kid be irreplaceable, which she is, it becomes difficult for admissions to say no.

As parents you could be much more helpful earlier in the process. In fact, long before any mention of the essay.

Now that you have permission, let's find out how.

Part 1 - CONFESSIONS

JOHN DEWIS

1. Gamer

I got a phone call from a mother eager for me to talk her son out of writing about video games. Her feeling was: He's such a good kid, and they're not going to know it if he writes about Xbox!

Her anxiety about Jake's essay was fueled by her fear that video games had taken over his life, and she was powerless to bring him back. Mom blamed Jake's gaming on her divorce and moving Jake across the country with her. There's already a lot going on here, and Jake's essay has become a big stress. They can't discuss it, and that's why she's calling me.

Mom's fear is corroborated by a friend in admissions at a local college who says, "We are so nervous about gaming culture here that it's hard to imagine a gaming essay making it past the first round." She also says, "We spend enough time as an administration worried about preventing any active shooter scenarios, that the mention of a first-person shooter game will be a red flag that keeps him out."

I believe these are true statements from admissions and legitimate fears from Mom. But what are they about? A topic. I'm going to spend time throughout this book convincing you there is no such thing. And if you do happen to discover a "topic" it doesn't necessarily mean you are any closer to you. To put it simply: people are not topics.

And if you do end up discovering your essay is "about" something, it shouldn't start out knowing that. For Jake, all we can say so far is that for a hypothetical essay about gaming, there are reasons to worry. But what about Jake's actual essay, or Jake's actual gaming, or for that matter Jake?

I ask Mom, "Does Jake's essay confirm your worst fears?" And she replies, "Luckily he hasn't written it yet!" Expert advice and parental fear have conspired to prevent Jake from writing his essay.

How do I help Jake? First, I make no assumptions about topics, given that I think they are phantoms. All I know is, it sounds like Jake likes video games. Isn't it nice to have something to talk about? Jake is the one who starts our conversation:

"My mom won't let me write about video games."
I laugh. We both laugh.
"What do you want to write about?"
"Video games!"
"Well, she's paying me to help you, and I'm committed to her getting her money's worth, so how about you write it!"
"How?"
"Well, what do you like about video games?"

Jake and I are on Zoom and hovering over the same Google doc called "JAKE!" We take turns writing down everything he says. He corrects my spelling and lack of punctuation; at the speed he is talking, I am a mediocre voice-to-text machine. There is a lot of laughter. He is relieved to be writing about something he thinks about.

When he stops, if it looks like he's thinking, I don't say anything. And then he keeps explaining and writing. If he stops and looks at me, I ask him another question. He is in charge of this conversation, but we are both enjoying it.

4

You might be wondering: this all sounds lovely, but are his answers to these questions his college essay? The short answer is yes. Among the 2000 words it takes him to answer these questions are indeed the 650 that do the job.

How is that possible? Over the course of this book, I hope it will become clear that it is not only possible but inevitable. Making this seem anything but mystical requires a shift in what we think writing is.

If we think writing is a carefully crafted form of communication arguing a position of certainty, then we are shocked when this one-hour conversation yields his essay. If instead we imagine writing as a form of thinking aloud or in dialogue with yourself, then it's no surprise.

My questions are not random, and they are not a questionnaire. They are based on whatever he just said. They are actual questions that have arisen in my effort to hear and understand Jake. Sometimes I ask aloud and he answers and writes. Sometimes I just write my questions in our shared Google doc, and he writes. Questions like:

Which video game?
Why do you like that one?
When did you first play it?
When did it become your favorite?
Which moment?
Like when?
I can't picture it; where were you headed exactly in the fortress?
What did you do when that happened?
If you had that same moment again, what would you do differently?
If you were the video game maker, what would you make happen instead?
Well then what choices would you provide so that something else happened?

And even:
What does your mother hate most about that?
Why does she think so?

What do you tell her?
What would you tell her?
What doesn't she quite understand?
What would make her change her mind?

And also:
Is there anything at all worrisome about that?
Is there something really good about that?
Has knowing that made you do anything different in the world outside of gaming?
If you had to describe that as a skill, how would you describe it?
How would you teach it?
Have you learned anything bad from video games?
Would there have been any way for you to learn that outside of that game?

These questions all have something in common:

1) They are not brilliant: they require no knowledge of video games, Jake, or anything else.
2) They are not general: they must be specific because they are asked to find something out.
3) They are not judgy: my positive or negative feelings about video games are not relevant.
4) They are not about his essay: they seek only Jake's own experience and thoughts.

I've translated these features of the best questions into four *Rules of Engagement.*

1) Be ignorant.
2) Be specific.
3) Don't be judgy.
4) Don't mention the essay.

The key is listening. Honest, deep, patient, present, and engaged listening. For many parents this requires a change in tack for the simple reason that you already know your kid. It can be hard to listen with fresh ears.

Jake trusts that I'm listening by observing me listen. Kids have already learned they can't just assume it. Establishing trust is not some grave series of exchanges to size each other up. He's not trusting me to pack his parachute or guide him through the underworld.

In other words, the relationship is not complicated even though the material is. We are willing to have fun wondering about things together. It's often hilarious. There can also be tears. It depends on what your kid discovers.

Sooner or later Jake is talking about Vermont, because he says things about video games that take him back to the woods. And then, a simple question, and he writes for ten minutes without stopping:

"What do you miss most about living in Vermont?"

> *The first trail I cut on my parents' land was through a dense patch of pine trees parallel to our driveway. I found an abandoned bathtub and discarded vehicle parts as I raked away dry leaves and pine needles. I used this same trail later to get to the tree house I built with my dad. I made trails in all directions into different types of forests: one to a small creek whose flow I manipulated with pipes and rocks, another to a swamp of spindly young oaks, and a third to an old growth area of firs choked with thick, non-native dark red vines. I was a pioneer of my own backyard and I built trails to understand the woods and to bring order to the random patterns of the forest. After my family moved to Southern California those trails went from the forest and into the digital world.*

What advice could I have given Jake to produce the above paragraph? What topic? What strategy? What lesson? None. The trail into his mind cannot start where it ends.

These questions would <u>not</u> work:

1) *Video games are too scary; why not write about something similar but different?*

2) *Why not write about your childhood before video games were part of your life?*

3) *Instead of video games, can you write about the divorce, move, and your dad?*

These questions reflect an agenda. Each of them violates some or all the *Rules of Engagement.* You might notice, however, that Jake ends up fulfilling all three of these unfair wishes in the first paragraph, entirely of his own volition.

1) He writes about the woods as similar to video games.

2) He writes about his childhood before video games.

3) He writes about his move to Long Beach and his dad in Vermont.

How did it happen?

It appears these questions are just as unfair for him to avoid as they are for me to ask. Have faith that the things that matter will turn up because they must, rather than because you said so.

The simple advice here to parents is *just say yes.*

If his essay is about how exciting it is to be a first-person shooter, which brings real clarity to the world, then I would need to have a conversation with his mother about getting him a therapist. I'm not being funny about that. It would be irresponsible not to get him help.

But if his mother says *He's such a good kid,* and then when I meet him on Zoom it appears to be true, then I have faith that if he is allowed to discuss what matters to him, it cannot help but reveal his goodness.

As a parent you are even better positioned to have faith in this. If you think video games are a blemish on a shiny kid, then go for the blemish and see if your kid survives. Even better, don't look for evidence that your kid is blemished or shiny, just look for evidence of your kid.

Here's his second paragraph:

> *"Grenade rolls down a hill" is a phrase my best friend and I coined from a game which gives us enough freedom to get in harm's way. Many games are based on conflict, but few let you put yourself in awkward, unforeseen situations. I threw a (virtual) grenade a little too low, and it landed-- pin-out-- above me on a slope and began to roll back down! I had been in full control of the situation, but now I was on a desperate escape through the dark jungle. This loss of power was not scripted-- I found myself developing a new story and living by my wits alone. I miss walking too far off the trail and the freedom of the forest. Now, the wild green landscapes I experience on screen in vast open-ended games help make up for the endless concrete of L.A. County, where the streets are all pre-explored.*

This didn't come right after his first paragraph in the Google doc. He wrote it earlier in response to my question about what moments of gaming he relishes most. But he found copying and pasting it right after revisiting the woods in his old back yard works.

Too scary to mention a grenade? The grenade is the thing that puts him in harm's way, which prompts him to realize what he likes most specifically about gaming. So, no. I don't ignore his mother's anxiety; I get him to talk about it.

One of my rules in *Hack the College Essay* is to explore the other side. I never had to ask Jake to do it because the other side was already alive and kicking. The other side might have been something like *What do critics of video games fear most?* or *What do most people fail to understand about video games?* Here's what he wrote without prompt:

Critics of video game culture have a point: the community of "Halo" has collectively wasted 235,182 years in twelve years, while Peter Molyneux's "Curiosity" divides players by selling a $10,000 pickaxe to mine a large rock for treasure. Not to mention the virtual death toll, which would be highly disturbing. But these numbers are inspiring to me: all these devoted players are waiting, whether they know it or not, to be channeled into something useful. How much water could you desalinate with the energy spent on shooting virtual avatars? I want to change the structure of videogame culture into a productive cooperative venture.

His critique of gaming isn't too far from his mom's. I give Mom credit for knowing her son and getting me to help. She doesn't know how fun it was.

Jake goes on to talk about a gaming club he founded at school and the way creative games might foster social movements. He not only got in everywhere he applied—he got a full ride to his first-choice, University of Vermont.

Saying yes no matter what might sound undisciplined and wishy-washy. On the contrary, saying yes is a highly disciplined form of investigation that lets a kid think whatever he thinks and then spend time figuring out why.

Remember Mom blamed her divorce and move cross country for Jake's gaming. That's what made the essay fraught. But it's also what made it the essay that got him in: in just a few minutes of honest conversation Jake takes us straight to Vermont where he built a treehouse with his father.

It takes just a few more sentences to see there's no stress here and that no one is at the mercy of a "topic." Could Jake's mom have prompted him to write the essay he needed to? I think so. It would have started by saying *yes*.

2. The Demonstration Trap

S am didn't start out writing about a fart. He wrote his first essay about depression and how playing with Legos helps him relax. The essay was depressing and made Sam sound like he'd resorted to playing alone with the toys of his childhood.

His college counselor loved it. She thought the essay was deep, sensitive, searching, hopeful, and showed real maturity and a willingness to be vulnerable. I thought it sounded like the work of an aspiring psychopath.

The reason I don't feel bad judging this work harshly is that it wasn't technically Sam's. He wrote it "under the influence of the college essay." You should never write under the influence of the college essay, because it will end up sounding like a college essay.

The point is that it sounded nothing like Sam. These essays often drive parents to contact me. You know something is wrong but aren't sure how to fix it.

Here's Sam's opening paragraph:

> *To me, anxiety is like a backpack, the more you carry and hold inside of it without organization, the*

more you'll see yourself suffer from the weight. In Junior year, my backpack was always stuffed, as I had binders, packets, textbooks, and essays constantly occupying the space inside of it. But there was more than just the increased workload of school inside, there was this intense pressure and the constant fighting around my household that I had to carry everywhere inside, and because I had to carry this bag everywhere I went, I struggled to find an environment of solace. Wherever I was, I felt all the weight stuffed in this backpack I was carrying to school and back home with me. The hardest part was that I couldn't find a place to empty this backpack of mine, so I was forced to carry it everywhere. I began to look for ways to release stress and anxiety, whether it was meditation or working out after school, none of them really seemed to treat this problem the way I thought they would. So, I began to think about my childhood, which was a much simpler time, and the things that possibly would have brought me comfort or peace back then. Immediately, I thought of toys. When I was younger, I loved to build Legos and create these buildings with them. In that case, I thought to myself: Will Legos really help me deal with stress? As funny and child-like as it sounds, it worked. I found Legos in the school library and began to play with them before my test. For the first time in years, I realized I wasn't nervous for the exam. Somehow, the Legos had released the feeling of overwhelming emotions and anxiety during times when I felt them the most.

Where does a doozy like this go? Admissions has moved on. But just in case you're interested:

Every time I played with the Legos, I was able to dump this backpack of anxiety and focus on building. When building, I felt that it was helping me move forward, stopping me from getting my head stuck on the issues at home or school that were bothering me. Whether I was building a spaceship or a tower, I had forgotten about all this anxiety and issues that flooded my mind. Although using Legos as therapy was silly and unorthodox, it taught me that when I'm solving a problem whether it's in real life or building, I'm able to put together the pieces and jumbled thoughts while also keeping at a controlled pace. The Legos help me move forward, stopping me from getting my head stuck on other issues bothering me. It reminded me that I could truly build my way out of things. Not only could I better control my anxiety and begin moving forward, but it gave me a sense of control that the world doesn't. My family has always been in a state of chaos and being able to design my own cities, environments, and line up my stormtroopers allows me to quite literally control my own little empire. When building, it fills me with a sense of emotional freedom that I find hard to obtain. Through this strange, yet helpful technique I developed to lower my anxiety, I really began to feel changes in the way I handled stressful situations. Now, completely stress free, I was able to really start focusing on the positives. And now, after this small obsession with a kid's toy, I can say that my backpack feels lighter, and so I am encouraged to keep building.

What kind of advice prompted it? When you're under the influence, it's not easy to tell. It might be a well-meaning counselor, or it might be what students assume they need to write to demonstrate maturity and depth.

It's what I call the Demonstration Trap.

Sam gave me permission to include it here because he isn't afraid anyone will mistake it for him. This is the same reason it wouldn't work for admissions.

Students fall into the Demonstration Trap for another reason, too: admissions asks for it. They provide prompts like *Tell us about a problem that you overcame.* Students then feel pressure to demonstrate a problem and that they overcame it.

How do these requests take students so far from the truth? Sometimes by creating anxiety that my problem isn't big enough. Many students hope embellishing a minor problem will make it worth overcoming.

Sam's Lego essay just presents the idea of a problem. Is the problem too much homework? Argumentative parents? Test anxiety? He tries them all on for size and then chooses anxiety because it's the problem most capable of being solved with Legos.

Parents are often delighted to help their kid find a problem that will make him the hero of the essay. This means you play into the Demonstration Trap. I hear parents coax their kids into sharing stories of overcoming hardship:

1) *Remember at scout camp when you were afraid to scale the wall but then did it?*

2) *Remember how hard you worked to win the science prize with your Tesla coil?*

3) *Remember in soccer when you nursed your ACL tear back in time to win States?*

These are fair things to write about, and parents can jog the memory of their kids. But usually struggles overcome head straight into the Demonstration Trap because they are remembered specifically to show something. Your kid is replaced by perseverance, and we never get to know her.

Try turning each suggestion above into a real question:

1) *How did you end up scaling the wall at scout camp?*

2) *Why were you so committed to building the Tesla coil and why for so long?*

3) *Has your ACL tear changed the way you play soccer?*

These work better because we don't know where they go. We don't know what, if anything, they might demonstrate. Otherwise, you are writing the conclusion first and bending the facts to support it.

Parents are not always midwives to bullshit. Sometimes you are well aware something is bullshit but aren't sure how to call it out! The same strategy works in both cases: Instead of asking your kid to demonstrate something, ask him to help you figure something out.

If you ask real questions, the truth has a way of revealing itself.

> *What specific Lego construction you built makes you most proud?*
> *What do your parents argue about most?*
> *What one thing in your backpack would you keep if it were on fire?*
> *How much does your backpack actually weigh?*
> *Where did you learn to meditate?*
> *When was the moment you realized that the Legos were working?*

Sam couldn't answer any of these questions. This is proof it wasn't Sam. It wasn't plagiarized; it was just fiction spun from a few stray childhood facts. He thought it sounded deep, and a combination of expert advice and parental restraint helped him think he had succeeded.

These are persistent unwritten rules of the college essay, and you are well warned <u>not</u> to follow them:

> *"Allow yourself to be vulnerable."*
> *"Pick a simple topic that will make a great metaphor for life."*
> *"Make your interests relatable by grounding them in your emotions."*

I had the benefit of working with Sam since he was in seventh grade. I knew he was talented, hilarious, sensitive, and wise. How can we learn those things without demonstrating them?

Ask Sam questions that will help him think. Usually something in an essay already written can springboard to the actual essay, but I couldn't see it. I started asking him questions to get him to reflect on his actual life.

What's one thing you have memorized by heart?
When, how, and why?
What's the most important past or future day of your life?
What's the most embarrassing moment of your life so far?
When was the time you most changed your mind about something?
What moment from history would you most like to live in?
What historical person would you most like to meet?
What is the single most important thing you ever learned in school?
What is the thing you've learned that surprised you most?
If school were all one subject, which would you want it to be?
Do you have a favorite book and why? Favorite movie and why?
Tell one great lie about yourself that you wish were true?
Tell one great truth about yourself that you wish were a lie?
How would your best friend write your epitaph?
How would your worst enemy write your epitaph?
How would you write your epitaph?
Did you ever get punched, punch someone, or wish you had?
What is your essential contradiction?
What is your least popular opinion?
What opinion of yours is the one shared by the fewest other people?
What is something that you think is true that you can't prove?
What is something everyone thinks is true that you're sure is false?
What one page would you read aloud from your autobiography?

I ask the last one and he starts to laugh.

"You've got to share what you just thought of."

"Ok sure I'll share it but it's not for the college essay."

"Perfect. What was it?"

"It was the time a guy farted loudly in the bathroom at the Arclight."

"Tell it!"

"I ran to the Arclight bathroom before Star Wars Episode Seven, and you know how it's always really crowded just before the film starts, well this guy let out an enormous fart. My friends and I still laugh about it."

Even when the answer seems like *no* it's worth seeing where *yes* takes him. I asked him questions and he wrote it all down. The essay was done in an hour, except the first paragraph, which came later. He loved his story, but he wasn't sure it was kosher.

"John, do you think there's a way to tell this story without the fart?"

"Sam, do you think there's a way to tell this story without the fart?"

"I'm sorry but I just don't see any way around it."

"So why not say that?"

"You mean maybe if I word it carefully, I won't offend anyone?"

"So why not say that?"

"And if I explain that this story makes me laugh but also makes me think a lot about humor?"

"So why not say that?"

I realize there's a fine line between silliness and maturity, and this story embarks on that theme. So, I'm hoping if I word this story the right way you will understand its importance and value, not only to me, but to society, and that you will not be offended at all that it contains a "fart." I see no way around it; this was a fart that made me rethink the way people should interact, and as a storyteller, it allowed me to see humanity in even the silliest of moments.

So, let's take it from the beginning: my friends and I were at the Arclight Movie theatre in Hollywood to watch Star Wars Episode Seven, and as usual, we decided to take a trip to the bathroom before the film. The film was sold out and the bathroom was completely packed. When we went to wash our hands, I could feel the bathroom bustling with excitement, as people discussed this much-anticipated film. I could

*also hear people arguing over whether Luke
Skywalker would show up in the film. The whole
bathroom got involved by giving their theories of Luke:
Would he turn up? Would he go to the dark side?
Was he the father of Rey? The arguments got heated
and people shut rival theories down, and it seemed that
people were more focused on each other's differences
rather than their shared excitement for the film.*

*As I was washing my hands and listening to the
banter, the room went silent for a split second, and in
that split second, there was a loud fart. Stunned, my
friends, the strangers in the bathroom, and I all looked
at each other with the expressions of, "Did you hear
that?!" After what seemed to be a long, awkward
silence, the man who farted exclaimed, "How'd you
like that?" The bathroom erupted into laughter.
Although the source of insight is unorthodox, this
struck me as very significant, as I saw everyone put
aside their differences and enjoy each other's laughter
for a moment.*

College counselors have real value and plenty of good advice. They are also generally stressed out. Sam's college counselor said she simply could not approve this essay. A fart shows immaturity and a lack of seriousness. Too risky.

She might be right about farts, but we're talking about a specific fart from a specific day in a specific place. Is this something she feels about farts generally or about this specific fart?

Sam was applying early to NYU's competitive undergraduate film program at Tisch. I thought it was perfect, if Sam did, and it was really his own decision to make.

Sam's parents broke the deadlock. They loved it and thought it was *so Sam!* He apologized to his counselor and sent it. He got in early to Tisch at NYU and I guarantee they read it aloud and passed it around the admissions table.

One odd thing I notice now from Sam's first essay is that he describes his Lego therapy as "silly and unorthodox." These are the same words he uses to describe his fart story. It's conceivable Sam was hiding there after all, and if we asked him to choose the silliest and most unorthodox thing he ever experienced, it might have yielded the fart.

My friends and I often remember this moment together and laugh, not only because it is such a fun story to tell, but because it can also relate to how desperately this feeling of connection is needed in America right now. In a time where conflicting values are all we seem to focus on, we find ourselves tearing each other apart over the differences of our beliefs. The current political climate has split people into far right and far left, and it means we don't really know how to argue meaningfully with each other anymore. In a way to de-objectify the fart the best I can, I feel like America needs a fart right now, something to laugh over, something to bring us together, something to put things in perspective, something that builds community and comfort through humor. In this moment I also felt connected with complete strangers. Everyone stopped fighting over theories of Luke Skywalker and laughed freely and uncontrollably. I even saw one man put his hand on the shoulder of another, acknowledging this connection. The bathroom is a place where we tend to completely avoid strangers, even eye-contact, and this small moment of camaraderie was able to affect everyone by bringing us all together to put aside our opinions and focus on similarities.

We have more in common with strangers than we think. I believe that everyone has their own set of values, but if they don't match, we shouldn't assume someone is wrong. Who would've known that a fart could have made a bathroom of some thirty-odd strangers bond? Similarly, it is the small moments of humanity and the power to bring people like this that have made me want to become a filmmaker. The ability to share beautiful moments of humanity are the reasons I love to tell stories, and the feeling of knowing that I am able to let people forget about their conflicts with each other for that small period of time, brings me the most joy.

My only criticism is that Sam goes to such lengths to explain the lesson. Typically, the lesson speaks for itself. As I say elsewhere, lessons are universal, so they use up time when we could get to know Sam.

I think it's okay because he never grandstands the lesson; he just tells what the fart made him think. The lesson also has several dimensions, including a timely non-partisan comment on our then presidential election.

What's the advice for parents? First, your kid is in the driver's seat. If he latches onto something, let him. But isn't this just another version of just say yes? And didn't that fail here, since his first impulse was to write about depression and Legos?

Well, yes and yes. The harder lesson here is: how to tell your kid his essay is bullshit.

You might have thought my value was that you could happily let a third party deliver the news. Now you know the answer: you don't have to tell him. If the essay is bullshit, it doesn't need you or me to say so. It will stink when we get close to it. So that is exactly what we do.

Parents are good at knowing when something is not quite right. Kudos to Sam's parents for doing something about it, even though Sam considered the work deep and mature.

Parents are also good at knowing when something is strangely perfect. Kudos to Sam's parents again for endorsing his true work, against the experts.

I don't spend time convincing a student of something self-evident. I just ask questions like those above. He sees the first essay isn't his because it has no details specific to him. Strictly *college essay-ese.* The only thing common to stress and Legos is every kid on the planet.

I have had students who write about Legos, but you need to ask enough annoying questions so your kid's Legos couldn't be anyone else's. Like, "What's the best thing you ever made out of Legos?" If the answer is, "Our Lego fortress had no discernible color scheme because my brother and I were in such a rush to build it" then we're onto something. That Lego kid got a scholarship to UVA in the school of engineering.

3. Bitcoin Miner

Students tell me they like it in *Hack the College Essay* when I hold feet to the fire. They know discomfort is a route to transformation and helps admissions get to know them. But students often choose something that sounds uncomfortable over something that is uncomfortable.

Hardship is most easily demonstrated physically. Which is why many essays start like a Rocky montage: beads of sweat, gritted teeth, and tensed muscles.

Now you know the goal is not to demonstrate. There are only so many ways to throw the body into discomfort, and much of life is spent avoiding them.

Hardship that stands a better chance of being specific to you is mental. It's born of confusion, frustration, or error. Mental discomfort enjoys an infinite landscape of possibility, and if you get specific enough you can find your very own.

Often that discomfort is ethical. Consider Evan's opening 200 words:

> *Increasingly everything from detergent to batteries to toiletries are clicked on and delivered to our doorstep. Like so many families, mine is dependent on*

Amazon, even though one fateful day it nearly bankrupted us. In 8th grade, after years of using my computer to play games, jailbreak iPhones, and create simple programs, I finally realized that technology could be used to make money- easy money. I started by earning ad revenue by redirecting fake traffic to websites, but I realized that my "get rich quick" schemes were actually only slowly earning me pocket change.

During this same time, Bitcoin was steadily increasing in both popularity and value. I saw this as the holy grail of earning passive income with a computer, but my laptop didn't have enough power to mine Bitcoins.

Ding! A "million-dollar" idea struck me. Armed with an empty Visa gift card and the infallible knowledge that they can't charge money on a card that had nothing on it, I set off to mine Bitcoins on Amazon's Virtual Private Servers. After a month, I received the first invoice for $10,000- a hilariously large number that they could not possibly expect me to pay. My friends quipped that Amazon was going to haul me off to jail for my debts, but I brushed it off because I knew that was impossible; I was using the oldest loophole in the books- I pretended I didn't see the bills.

If you cheat, and you've made the bold choice to talk about it in your essay, you can't just cross your fingers and hope we won't judge you.

Should he scrap it?

You know by now Evan doesn't need a better "topic." He has real facts that matter to him and a real ability to spit them out. Evan also reports this is the most significant thing that ever happened to him.

It's a great story that captures our attention, but the essay begun above will keep him out. Not the facts themselves, but that we see him scheme for so long without worry. It's a problem of tone, and it's not easy to help Evan see it or solve it. This is an example of someone who is in terrific command of an essay, but where 10% off the mark will sink him.

The problem is that he never deals openly with how he feels about his error or how he learned it was wrong. It's like a pat apology: if you don't say what you're sorry about, we don't buy it.

You might think less is best: gloss over the self-incriminating bits and get to the hard lesson. Experience tells me this will make it sound like he's hiding something. This is because he will be hiding something.

As his parent you might be tempted to tell him, "This essay makes you sound dishonest." Experience tells me this will make him feel bad, shut down, scrap it, and start fresh with a Rocky montage.

My own impulse might be counterintuitive: *Why not reveal more?* Good questions will help him get there, but they aren't questions to scribble in the margin and send back. They require conversation.

Revealing more won't make his essay too long, but it might get long before it gets short. He'll have more details from which to choose his final 650 words, and that's a good thing. Words often balloon to 2000 to reveal the best 650.

Our conversation starts from the beginning. Evan sounds like a victim of Amazon rather than a guy who rang up a bill he couldn't pay. Accountability begins by owning exactly what he did. I ask questions to specify when, how, and why.

1) *I don't understand the mechanics; why was this all so expensive?*
2) *What's great about passive income for you more than for others?*
3) *How long before you saw the first bill?*
4) *Did you ever earn as much as quickly as you say you wanted?*
5) *How does it feel to have ignored requests for payment?*
6) *Did $10,000 seem a "hilariously large number" then or now?*

Each of these questions can be translated into a rule for students:

1) Explain what you did in the necessary level of detail.
2) Cut the first paragraph if the story is clear without it.
3) Let things happen in the order they happened.
4) Prioritize whatever changed you most.
5) Describe your current self in ways that make you proud.
6) Distinguish between past and present thoughts.

It's not incumbent upon you or me to teach him the rules. He can find them if he wants in *Hack the College Essay.* I include them here to help you find the best questions.

Once Evan answers the questions above, his essay is indeed 2000 words, and he's miffed our conversation has taken him off course. How will he include it all?

He won't.

First, I ask him to take a breath with me. I am not a psychologist, but I've seen thousands of students in a full array of emotional states. Pausing and breathing slowly and deeply is a great way to calm down. In an exercise that involves a lot of words, mere breath is happily wordless. We breathe exaggeratedly and after our third exhale we laugh.

"Your essay is already there," I tell him. "You're 90% done, or more." He likes the sound of that.

"Read your doc from the top and highlight in some color whatever you think is most necessary or true." It takes him about three minutes.

"Nice choices. Now copy and paste all the highlighted stuff to the top of the doc."

He knows his best material better than I do, although much is determined logically by the work itself. It includes only the details required to understand his error and what they make him think. These are the parts no one else could say.

I watch him meticulously highlight half-sentence here, a string of sentences there. He jams things together and puts in the punctuation that makes it sensible. He makes a few paragraph breaks. He looks happy. Here's how he tells it:

When I started 8th grade, Bitcoin was front-page news, and I saw it as the holy grail of passive income: simply let a computer run a mining program that opens the market of foreign exchange. There was just one problem: with my own laptop, the cost of electricity required would offset any money that I could make.

A "million-dollar" idea struck me. Armed with a Visa gift card, I set off to mine Bitcoins on Amazon's Virtual Private Servers. I could use their free trial, and once it expired, my subscription would be cancelled. When I signed in, I realized my account wasn't limited to one server; I could use as many servers as I wanted before they closed my account. I installed the mining software on all the servers, and it seemed like I was off to the races.

A month later, I received the first $10,000 invoice. My friends joked that Amazon was going to haul me off to jail. I ignored the bills hoping they would resolve themselves. By the time I received the third invoice, however, I had a feeling I was in trouble. I hoped Amazon would shut down my account, but it was still very open, and the bill continued to grow with compounding overtime fees. I showed my dad, hoping he would assure me they would stop, but, as we examined the mounting bills, the gravity of the situation hit me. The bill was real, the servers are expensive, and I realized just how badly I messed up.

I called Amazon customer support in a panic. I felt like I was pleading for my life: "Hi, my name is Evan Shields and I messed up big time. I owe $25,000 and I'm an 8th grader. Please help me." The support representative paused, "I'm going to elevate this issue to my supervisor. Thank you for

*calling." She gave me a support ticket and told me to
check my email for updates.*

*Three months later, the bill was just over
$185,000. When I was out with friends, I calculated
my bill in terms of my regular purchases: 32,128
packs of gummy bears; 80,879 Cokes; 29,090 slices
of pizza. I finally received a call from an unknown
number in California. It was the Amazon
representative. The issue was resolved. They were not
going to commandeer the money or lock me in the
server room as an indentured servant. The nightmare
was over. I don't know exactly why they let me off the
hook. Maybe they thought sticking a 13-year-old with
a bill meant for large corporations would be a PR
nightmare; maybe a higher up at Amazon was
thankful I exposed a policy flaw before hackers
noticed.*

He's not done yet, but in this version Evan dives into the important facts without delay. He resists the temptation to set the scene in ways that merely describe what we know, like that Amazon has changed how we shop or that passive income is nice. Those are distractions.

Remember after our first hour talking and writing, Evan was worried he'd written too much. Notice how too much ends up being more efficient: in the old version it took him 150 words to get to his million-dollar idea; in the new version it takes just 50.

He also tones down the caricature of his relationship with money, but without eliminating his desire for it. Self-caricature is demeaning; it's also evasive. It's an avatar. If he cuts it, he'll discover the harder work of self-reflection.

Evan stops dancing around the thornier facts and just says it: he took advantage of free trials and installed software on multiple servers. This is more explanation than he thought he had room for, but he needs this level of detail to describe the error.

If we see precisely how his mind was working, we have a better chance of sympathizing. Evan is a sharp, articulate, focused, and enthusiastic student, and the connection between technology and scalable wealth is real. If the essay ended here, however, this would just be a cautionary tale. Evan wants to be a valuable member of the freshman class.

One question I often ask students is simply, "How do you feel?" This is not a soft question. I'm not checking in to make sure they aren't experiencing discomfort. I'm making sure they have a chance to sit with discomfort long enough to discover its effect on them. Something most of us have learned to avoid.

My question usually follows a delivery of facts like those above. We have a better chance of understanding feelings once we fully grasp the situation. How do you interview for a feeling? Something like this:

"How did this make you feel?"
"That I got caught?"
"Sure."
"I'm glad I was young enough that they took pity on me."
"That sounds like how you felt about being let off the hook, not how you felt about getting caught."
"I'm glad I learned that just because something is simple to do doesn't make it safe or right."
"What an amazing thing to learn. Still, this sounds like something you're glad about now, but what was it like at the time?"
"I lived in fear for months until it was resolved."
"Why?"
"I was afraid I had bankrupted my family."
"Why?"
"They've given me everything, including education, and I went and misused it."
"And how does that make you feel?"
"I'm mortified."

The tears arrived on *They've given me everything*. It's not my aim for him to cry, but sometimes that's what happens when we stumble onto the truth. He can feel good that he found something meaningful enough to produce tears.

I am also not fishing for "mortified" as the feeling to find. I had no idea what it might be. But fear of punishment is different from fear of having done something wrong. I asked questions that aimed for the I-did-something-wrong part.

It turns out that for Evan the crime against Amazon entailed a more poignant crime against his parents. In his first stab was the crime sounded blessedly victimless. No wonder he seemed blithe.

Schools often promise to provide opportunities for failure. I get it. But one consequence of the rise of failure is that in our enthusiasm to embrace it we forget why it's valuable. We jump over the discomfort to celebrate the lesson, overlooking the reason the lesson is a lesson in the first place.

Discomfort is a repercussion of a moral failing, and it also might be a clue that there is one. Evan thought it was okay to sign up for server space with recurring payments on gift cards knowing they would expire. Even if failure has hidden virtues, you have to know this is a mistake long enough to yearn for them.

When I push him to talk about this part it makes him anxious. He feels it. He hears his own responses to my questions and is eager to get them in.

> *I am mortified that I almost bankrupted my family, not to mention the worry that I set off on the wrong path with technology. In a way my parents were impressed that I was capable of getting into trouble with a multi-billion-dollar company, but they still wanted to teach me a lesson. My punishment was to create a list of ways to be entrepreneurial with technologies, but not to act on them without thinking through their ethical dimensions. I didn't think the punishment fit the crime; it was too lenient.*

When I got to high school, I learned to program, created my own applications, joined CyberPatriot, and learned that it's a lot more satisfying to create things with technology than to exploit the creations of others. I now have a website filled with apps that I designed to educate and entertain, including Machine Learning with Shakespeare and a study guide for AP Chemistry. My mistake didn't scare me away from being innovative, and I still push boundaries, but everything I make has the essential goal of providing value to others.

Most parents would have advised giving deceit a wide berth. Evan extracted deceit from the jaws of defeat and got into his first choice, Cornell.

We see how he did it, but how did we help?

First, we asked for the facts: what happened when. The more complicated, the more worth it. Once he finds the facts, he's got to deal with them.

Then, we asked questions to cut distracting facts from important ones. Discernment is especially necessary when the story is compromising. Non-judgy questions can still be persistent.

Finally, we asked what the facts made him feel. His true feelings about the most difficult facts convince us we are not dealing with a cyber-criminal.

What did we *not* do?

We never asked him to write a new essay, tone down his humor, soften the error, change his attitude, use better words, describe things using more senses, set the scene, dramatize the fear, or tie a bow.

We also never asked for an introduction or conclusion. Those are about the essay rather than about him. Does his essay have an intro and conclusion?

Depends on what you think they are. The essay follows linear time: the first paragraph says what he wanted to do, and the last paragraph what he went on to do. No preamble and no summing up.

We also never asked for a lesson, even though they are there for the taking. Instead of belaboring lessons, he helps us understand something subtle and true: the new Evan is similar in some ways but different in others to the old Evan. His reflection is honest, thoughtful, and crisp. He looks us in the eye and tells us who he is.

Part 2 - AVATARS

JOHN DEWIS

4. How it Sounds if You (the Parent) Write It

We've seen essays that parents wouldn't write, couldn't write, and in one case didn't even want written. Sometimes parents are so invested in the essay, however, that they write it themselves.

I think it's uncommon and not deliberate. It happens out of love, empathy, urgency, frustration, excitability, and a dash of masochism. I've been doing this long enough that I can tell right away when a parent has written the essay. It sounds the way some parents think kids sound to themselves.

Here's a real one:

> *"Mom, I'll be right down!" I just couldn't leave the soldering iron, not right now, not when I was so close. I was using my Arduino to build an array of LED lights that would tell me when my package arrived at the front door. You could say I'm a computer nerd, but it's what I love. When I was five, I took my parents' computer apart to see how it worked.*

Several computers (and a weekend grounding) later,
I'm really what you might call a tinkerer.

The dead giveaway that Mom wrote it is that she's the first character in the story. If this describes an actual moment, the kid probably never noticed that she called him or how he replied. Or it happens so often that this is a general impression of life at home rather than a specific instance of it.

But Mom has a vision of her kid so lovingly steeped in what he loves that he doesn't care about dinner. Another line from the essay: "My mom calls me her little absent-minded professor." More accurately: "I call my son my little absent-minded professor."

I can appreciate the wish to reveal what your kid is not willing to reveal about himself. But oneself cannot easily be revealed by another.

It's wrong to write your kid's essay. And it's ineffective, even if you're a crafty writer. More importantly, and to the point of this book, it prevents you from providing actual help.

Here's what I hear from parents who write it:

1) *But I remember a lot of great stuff my kid has probably forgotten!*
2) *But she refuses to share all the best things about herself!*
3) *But this is the one thing she's never been able to do!*
4) *But my kid's writing is totally in the clouds!*
5) *But I know my kid better than a lot of people!*
6) *But I know my kid better than he knows himself!*

Luckily these claims don't need to be true to turn them into help. Start by flipping them into questions:

1) I wonder what great stuff she remembers that I've forgotten?
2) I wonder what she considers the best and worst things about herself?
3) I wonder what she'll discover she can do?

4) I wonder what she actually means by that?
5) I wonder what I've failed to understand about my kid?
6) I wonder how my kid seems to himself?

Each impulse to answer turns into an impulse to listen. To help with the college essay, you don't need to prove how well you know your kid. Better to assume you've never met her. That makes the exercise a chance to get to know her in a different way, which is what the essay is for admissions.

One of my advantages helping kids write is that I've usually only just met them. It makes me keenly interested in what they think and why, and it makes them willing to teach me.

Parents are sometimes under the unfair impression they must provide feedback, answers, or wisdom. You don't! Don't be so hard on yourself. If you adopt a genuine posture of curiosity and interest, rather than urgency and expertise, you are on your way to providing real help.

Instead of feedback think inquiry, instead of answers think listening, and instead of wisdom think presence. These are not big fancy things that require special knowledge or sophistication.

Nope: ---> Yup:
Urgency ---> Curiosity
Expertise ---> Interest
Feedback ---> Inquiry
Answers ---> Listening
Wisdom ---> Presence

The *Yups* might take practice. This is why good questions are better than good topics. Good questions put you in the habit of listening for whatever turns up.

How do you know if you're asking good questions? Here's an accidentally hapless question:

Why not write about math?

A suggestion like this has an unspoken half that gets said after your kid says no:

But you are so good at math, and you love it!

This might seem like a good icebreaker, but it's a conversation stopper.

If it results in writing, it might be about the time she won a prize. Fair and true, but it might not matter much to her or could go on her resumé. *Why not write about math* pushes your kid into the Demonstration Trap before she has a chance to think.

It also invites your kid to label herself. Even labels that seem accurate or flattering are problematic in the college essay:

As a person who likes math,
As a stressed-out junior starting BC Calc,
As someone for whom math always came easily,

I have a rule against starting a sentence with the word *As* because it sets up an effigy: a doll made roughly in the form of the person it represents.

There's no harm in burning an effigy, so that's what admissions does. You don't want your kid to be an example of a certain kind of kid, you want her to be herself and stand only for herself. That's the person on behalf of whom she is applying.

Why not write about math is also a question about the essay and its topic rather than about your kid. Plain and simple. It's administrative rather than investigative. It means that even if you're not actually writing the essay, it might still sound like it.

Nope: ---> Yup:
Supervise ---> Unearth

Suggest ---> Provoke
Control ---> Free
Govern ---> Unleash
Manage ---> Observe

Why not write about math is also a binary question. You might get *Yes okee* or *No thankee* and that's the end of it. If you're lucky you'll get *What do you mean?* because then you'll have to wonder.

Why not write about math is also really vague. Good news: there are lots of specific questions you can ask about both math and your kid.

What is math, anyway? is already a hard question even though it sounds simple. It might even be too hard. I mention it because it's something we assume we know when we say *But you love math!*

Is math a feature of the universe we discovered? A feature of the human mind at work in the universe? A collection of verifiable facts or a circular system of rules? Cold truth? Elegant fiction? We don't know what math is and nobody does. We should allow it to be mysterious before we allow it to be a topic.

Merriam Webster is entertainingly broad on math:

"The science of numbers and their operations (see OPERATION sense 5), interrelations, combinations, generalizations, and abstractions and of space (see SPACE entry 1 sense 7) configurations and their structure, measurement, transformations, and generalizations."

Wikipedia is disconcertingly blunt:

"Mathematics has no generally accepted definition."

Nobody needs to define math in a college essay, but trying would be more engaging than saying or showing that you're good at math.

The right math questions to ask your kid use math as the occasion for admissions to get to know her:

1) *When was the first time you thought you might really like math?*
2) *When was the first time you encountered a truly hard math problem?*
3) *When was the most fun you've ever had with math?*

If these don't seem right, you can start conversation the most honest way possible:

4) *I was about to say, "Why not write about math; you love math!" but then I thought to myself, "You seem to be great at math, but do you love it?"*

Or by latching onto an instance of math in her life:

5) *Remember when you got the highest score in class on that test— what was it testing?*
6) *What was the hardest question on the test, or was there a question you thought you got wrong but got right or thought you got right but got wrong?*
7) *Is there a kind of problem in math you do differently than other people do it?*

These stand the best chance of making math make her think about herself:

8) *Does the study of math make the world look different to you?*
9) *Do you do something other than math differently because of math?*
10) *What aspect of math makes the least sense to you?*

And to discover her own idiosyncratic love for it:

11) *Who is your favorite mathematician from the history of math?*
12) *What mathematical concept would you be most excited to teach me?*

13) *What would you change first about how math is taught if you were in charge?*

And the best follow-up questions:

14) *Why?*
15) *When was that most true?*
16) *How does that feel?*

These questions follow the *Rules of Engagement:* willfully ignorant, maniacally specific, blissfully not judgy, and painstakingly not about the essay.

One way to elicit maniacal specificity is to ask questions that contain superlatives: *first time, last time, most fun, most true, most wrong, most different, most surprising, favorite, funniest, scariest, worst, hardest, least, highest, best.*

Superlative questions tend to have just one answer. They pin down actual times, places, events, memories, things, people, thoughts, and feelings. Unlike being good at math, these things don't belong to any other person in the world and therefore no other applicant can share them.

Once parents embrace this style of questioning, however, sometimes you ask and retreat. You might think after a crackling question your kid should be left alone with her thoughts. Otherwise, your own further thoughts might influence her.

Not so!

A conversation is an exercise in mutual influence and discovery. Give her the chance to be alone if she wants or with you if she wants company. Sharing your own experiences can further an investigation, reveal something in common, or highlight a sharp difference. You are a human who knows and might have created the applicant. For the same reason that you can press all the wrong buttons, you are well positioned to jostle revelation.

But don't trick her into revealing something you know about her. Ask questions that give her the chance to discover something about herself. All the better if you learn something you didn't know.

If sharing your own thoughts leads you to say, "Now that I think of it, if I were you I would talk about x" then you unwittingly make the conversation unhelpful again. Phrases like this reinforce roles and thus role-playing: she is made to feel desperate and you are made to feel like a consultant. Or your kid decides you don't understand and should butt out!

We can see now that a Why-not-talk-about-x question is a just sneaky variation of an If-I-were-you assertion. Look closely at the phrase *If I were you.* Putting yourself in her shoes might sound empathetic to your ears. But it asks your kid to imagine what is most at odds with the job: that she is someone else. In this case, you.

Writing the essay only she could write is not the same as writing the essay she could write if only she were someone else. Liberating news for parents. Your own thoughts don't need to be on behalf of your kid. They get to be yours. As equals you are both entitled to share whatever you happen to think.

Your own thoughts can springboard real questions:

17) *I read the other day that a famous source of random numbers is not that random! Is it possible to generate a random number?*

18) *I read an obituary for a crazy guy from Princeton who discovered surreal numbers. Do you have any idea what those are?*

19) *I remember hearing that the Greeks had no need for zero because geometers have no use for zero length. Does math work without zero?*

20) *I don't use math at all in my job or life. Or do I? Should I?*

I have found tough or odd questions build confidence rather than sap it. They ask us to use our minds. They can result in the pleasure of reading an article together or her explaining something to you.

It doesn't take much to be a good conversationalist. Find out what's important to her. Learn something from her. It doesn't take long for her to say something staggering. But it need not be staggering. It might just be true, personal, or interesting. Have her write it down. It's that simple.

<u>Yup:</u> *Can you write that down, what you just said?*

And the reason I go to the trouble of writing that down for you, is that this clean direction is usually translated into something more complicated, and nothing gets written.

<u>Nope:</u>
You should consider writing your essay about that.
That sounds like a great topic to brainstorm.
That observation could conclude a great essay.
If I were you, I would absolutely run with that.

The reason to write it down is not to put it in your essay. The essay gets discovered after a series of true, personal, or interesting things get written down.

This chapter began with a parent's essay. Most agree that in addition to being unethical, it doesn't work. Very few parents, however, would question the value of routine forms of help like brainstorming, outlining, finding a topic, or remembering a hard lesson. Precisely because this help doesn't register as an ethical problem, we don't bother to ask if it poses a practical problem. It does.

Why? Because these are administrative forms of help meant to provide direction and structure, but the best essays live outside the structure. Boundaries dictate a sphere of thought and close paths of inquiry, rather than setting the mind free and seeing where it goes. They take your kid out of the driver's seat and set her up to write something that will please upper management but annoy admissions.

This macro-management is potentially more damaging to the essay than sitting down and writing it yourself! If the point of the essay were merely to demonstrate something about your kid, then an essay written by you or anyone capable of demonstrating something about your kid would do the job, ethical considerations aside. Provided it was true, we might not especially care who said it.

Admissions asks for recommendations from teachers and coaches that do just this. This is not what they want in the essay. The essay is a chance for your kid to cut through everything admissions has already seen and heard and present herself. If it requires anything at all, it requires your kid.

5. How it Sounds if the Counselor Writes it

Parents are not the only adults who take the hands-on approach. Noah's college counselor said his essay was too complicated and he should make it more conversational. That's a page from my book: complex thoughts require simple words. His counselor took the extra initiative to rewrite it as Noah might if he were willing to be conversational.

Here's the opening paragraph:

> *Stock photographs. We've all seen them: the smiling faces with too white teeth, the enthusiastic gestures and firm handshakes, the exaggerated expressions depicting every possible human emotion—all with the same brilliant white background. In the last two years, stock photographs have taken up residence in my subconscious, burrowing deep into the core of who I am and settling in for the long haul.*

Sounds like a stand-up routine, right? Some adults think when kids speak their minds they speak abruptly, like cartoon kids in a comic strip. Golly. If you work with kids, you know they are usually more Faulkner than Hemingway. I frequently tell students one verb replaces the work of three.

Notice there are no actual verbs here until the third sentence. Except in the stock phrase *We've all seen them,* where the subject is safely everyone in the world. To make up for it we get a string of verbals—words formed from verbs but not functioning as verbs. Most verbals are adjectives: smiling, exaggerated, depicting, burrowing, settling.

My objection, apart from that this paragraph was written by someone other than Noah, is that making it conversational just makes it strange. If a student writes something like this, I don't ask him to change his words; I ask questions that require specificity.

Which expression was most exaggerated?
Which emotion did it depict?

I had already spent one hour per week with Noah for three weeks, prompting him to talk about all kinds of experiences, including his photography project. I recognized the source material. How Noah first said it was the best way—from the source. He was upset about the rewrite, and so was his mother.

Here's what he asked:

"It doesn't sound like me, but is it better?"

By now I hope you recognize that beyond being heartbreaking, this question is illogical: the best essay for us to get to know him sounds like him.

Here's the second paragraph from his counselor. The facts are familiar, but the presentation new:

Let me get one thing straight: I am not obsessed with stock photographs but rather with the idea of them—the characteristics they are associated with and my relationship with those characteristics. The seed of my obsession was planted in the summer before my junior year, when I attended a photography program in New York. I was convinced that photography was my life passion, and I wanted to start pursuing it more seriously. As a final project, I had to create a series of self-portraits revealing a new understanding of myself to an audience. As a photographer, I like to be behind the camera, watching stories unfold before my eyes and capturing those stories. The notion of capturing my own story presented foreign territory. For days after the assignment was announced, I could not think of a single defining characteristic of mine that I could explore further. I would spend hours taking long walks or sitting at a desk with my computer watching the cursor blink slowly at the top of a blank page. This loss for words terrified me. Why was it so hard for me to articulate who I really was? Did I know? Would I ever know? A distressing experience, to say the least.

Noah's counselor uses sound principles but puts them to poor use. It's a great example of crafty help gone awry.

I knew a theater instructor at Harvard who used to tell students, "Your technique is showing." It was not a compliment. To put it simply for parents: don't translate your kid's work into something you think sounds better.

Why not? The effort to sound a certain way makes the writing inefficient, inhuman, and untrue. Admissions will reject it without taking time to figure out why. It'll just rub them the wrong way.

For us, it's worth seeing what went wrong. I'll identify the problem and a question that corrects it.

Problem: If we've all seen stock photos, then no need to spend time describing them.

Question: *Can you describe the photos you took of yourself and which one you like best?*

Problem: If you think a lot about stock photos, you don't need to tell us three different ways: taking up residence, burrowing, settling in. Is this an essay about a deer tick?

Question: *Can you tell us specifically where, when, and which photo took hold of you?*

Problem: Just using the phrase *the core of who I am* does not mean we get to know you.

Question: *Instead of saying <u>that</u> you think about stock photographs, can you tell us <u>what</u> you think about them?*

Problem: The first paragraph is told from the perspective of an inanimate object. Make yourself the subject of the sentence and tell the story from your own perspective.

Question: *When and why did you first think about a stock photo long after you looked at one?*

Problem: You don't need to say you are about to say something before you say it. When someone asks you how you are doing, you don't say, "I'm about to tell you how I'm doing, which is to say: just fine." You say, "Fine, thanks. How are you?" Otherwise, it sounds like you are not fine. In which case just say, "Terrible! Do you have a minute?" When you say, "I'm going to tell it to you straight," it sounds like you are about to lie.

Questions: *What was the actual feeling you had when you started looking closely at stock photos? Were the feelings about the people in them, about yourself, or about something else? Did the feelings change once you put yourself in the photos? Did the photos change?*

Each problem yields a question, and each question elicits specific facts and thoughts. In conversation with your kid, you can skip straight to the question.

Likewise, college admissions is not busy critiquing the essay. They're trying to get to know your kid. It's either working or not.

Here are five prohibitions inspired by the counselor. Do they help you generate questions?

1) No false subtlety.

No one thinks Noah loves stock photographs but hates the "idea" of them. To figure out why they unnerve him, Noah takes part in them. The faster he gets to that part the better.

2) No false psychology.

"Characteristics they are associated with and my relationship with those characteristics" is pretentious. Blech. Different aspects of stock photographs will reveal different thoughts. These actual thoughts will grab admissions in ways that mentioning the "subconscious" can only aspire. (And if something were subconscious, how would he know?)

3) No false sincerity.

"Let me get one thing straight" is a rhetorical posture. Coming clean in your essay is fine if it clears up misunderstanding. I had a student recently say,

> *John, I guess my big fear is that I don't want them to think this is an essay about ethnicity. Doing volunteer work in India was more effective than in Omaha, but it's not because I'm Indian; it's because there are fewer restrictions on the work in India.*

The above two sentences went straight into the essay, because the best way to explain it to the reader was the way she did to me.

4) No symbolic feelings.

Details about feelings should help us understand them. The counselor's details are merely symbolic of feelings, like a slowly blinking cursor on a blank page (which could be a stock photo). With only ninety seconds to tell us who you are, you don't want tedium and distress to be what we remember. Tell us what a moment of distress prompts you to do.

5) No figurative language.

Stylistic efforts don't deepen our understanding of the applicant. Phrases like *the seed was planted* and rhetorical questions like *would I ever know who I am?* might feel literary but they distract us from you.

I've turned each prohibition into an active rule:

1) Make real comparisons.
2) Be concrete.
3) Be sincere.
4) Find your actual feelings.
5) Phrase things directly.

Noah must translate from the twisted idiom of the college essay back into the honest voice of Noah.

> *There is a global extinction event every hundred million years. The one that killed the dinosaurs is the one people know about. Whether a mass algae bloom, volcano, or changing sea levels, something always ends up destroying the majority of life on Earth. I'm not saying we should worry about this, and I don't—the*

*next one will probably not happen in our lifetime. But
I think about it because I studied an asteroid called
1998 OH at the Summer Science Program in New
Mexico this past summer. Like most asteroids, 1998
OH is an ancient, floating, gyrating time capsule in
an elliptical orbit. What sets it apart is that it will
come within 0.03 AU of the Earth. This is far
enough that it shouldn't hit us, but close enough that
we need to keep an eye on it. Even tiny perturbations
in an asteroid's orbit can spiral into the sun, eject it in
a hyperbolic path out of the solar system, or send it
careening toward the Earth at 50,000 mph.*

His college counselor thought his asteroid was too nerdy
and his photography more humanizing. I say the only human
we care about is Noah. And he's at liberty to be nerdy. In his
own essay, photographs help him answer an asteroid
question:

*Given the likelihood of global extinction, how important is it that I
am who I am?*

His essay doesn't brag that at sixteen he was on a team to
track asteroids. He's telling us something rarely heard: how
his studies affect his life. We are more sympathetic to his
angst because we see where it comes from and what it drives
him to do.

*In an NYU program last summer, I created a
series of ten self-portraits depicting my life in the style
of stock photography. I wished to convey my fear of
relinquishing control of my life to a default or "stock"
existence—celebrating a birthday, eating a slice of
pizza, reading a book, all with the same bland, white
background. I didn't know what I wanted to do or
what I wanted to be, and I was scared that at some*

*point, I would be going through the motions of life
without developing an individual identity or purpose.*

Can you hear the difference between his counselor's voice
and his own? It takes Noah three sentences to describe his
photo project. His counselor turned it into a full-blown
existential crisis because she thought it was more engaging.

She might also think you shouldn't bite off too much in
one essay. People say you've got to make tough choices: *Is this
essay about photography or about an asteroid?* Students are
paralyzed by such false dilemmas.

If Noah has said what he wants about his photos, don't
squeeze 650 words out of it. Move on. *But if he moves onto
something new in the same essay, won't it just become a hodgepodge of
random stuff that will leave admissions scratching their heads?*

I had a student get into Duke, her first choice, with a
three-headed essay: the English composer Edgar Elgar, the
unsolved proof for the Theory of Quadrilaterals, and losing
her El Salvadorian grandmother to Covid. Already sounds
interesting.

The thing that unites these things is the thing we care
most about: Tati. If admissions wonders what unites them,
that's good, because it means Tati has them thinking about
Tati. It's a straight line from there to the freshman class.

Tati is not the only cellist who loves Elgar. But she is the
only quadrilateral-obsessed cellist whose late Salvadorian
grandmother told her something that makes her love Elgar.
Each one of us combines disparate things in one life and can
in one essay.

The lesson for parents: whatever your kid finds to answer
a good question will be what she needs. Let the question help
her determine what these things are rather than hoping a
brilliant essay topic will magically locate them.

In the land of the college essay, Tati might be tempted to
use the story of her grandmother's life and death to show that
Tati, too, is tough and not afraid of challenges. Since most of
us have survived the deaths of our grandmothers, and most

of us have embraced something challenging, this direction alone does not differentiate Tati. Better to ask:

Why do you love Elgar?
Which piece of music?
Which composer was your favorite before you knew Elgar?
Which piece of music?
What is this thing we know but can't prove about quadrilaterals?
Which is your favorite quadrilateral?
Which quadrilateral illustrates best the failure to prove the theorem?
What one thing did your grandmother hope most for you?
What one thing did your grandmother fear most on your behalf?
What one thing will you never understand about your grandmother?

Otherwise, no Tati and no college admission.

Noah can learn from Tati. He's stressed out and doesn't realize his mind is free to roam. Don't we think and talk in ways that grab what we need when we need it? We don't say, "Hey that's off-limits, can't you tell this conversation is about asteroids?"

We were talking about asteroids and how small changes in tack have huge effects over long distances, which is why we watch them closely. I asked if he had any other experiences where small things had big consequences.

On the river, small angles also matter. An imbalance in pressure from a single stroke can change a boat's line considerably, sending it towards the shore or around a bend in a wide and inefficient path. When I started rowing in the sixth grade, I competed in a lot of head races. Head races are long - usually about five or six kilometers - and a bad point can set you back by seconds or even minutes. Single sculling (one person) is the form of rowing I love most, because every movement is a reflection of the rower's skill. Small mistakes are magnified, and technical ability matters just as much as physical bulk. When I am moving a boat efficiently, it is a beautiful feeling. I am present and focused and can feel everything in the boat working the way it should. I have complete control and responsibility over where and how I go.

It's neither schlocky nor groundbreaking. It's sincere. We believe this is something Noah cares about, and it helps us get to know him.

So how do asteroids and rowers compare? They both move and can be steered, but in different ways. An asteroid is completely at the mercy of the gravitational fields permeating outer space. It drifts aimlessly until it hits something or is pulled in a new direction by a planet or star. A rower has agency. A little pressure on an oar can turn the boat in a completely different direction. A strong push from the legs can send it surging forward from a standstill. A flex of the arms can bring it to a shuddering stop.

In the past year I have realized that not knowing what I want to do with my life is okay; it does not mean I am floating aimlessly in the depths of space. Maybe I am just sitting on a single in a very large lake without a map. In the next four years, I will explore this lake and learn all it has to offer. When all is said and done, I can move a boat well. I just need to figure out where to point it.

Even though he doesn't know what he wants to do, we have confidence in Noah. He's thoughtful about his astronomy, rowing, and photography, and these disparate parts are reconciled in him. He's a scientist, an athlete, and an artist.

But he doesn't use these words to label himself. He just tells us stuff he thinks about and tries to figure out why it matters to him.

54

The aim of multifaceted Noah is *not* to show that he is multifaceted. And the aim of existential Noah is *not* to showcase his existential crisis. Noah discovers his own existential question on our watch, and the essay that gets him in tries to answer it. His college counselor thought he sounded nuts, but the University of Chicago was delighted.

JOHN DEWIS

6. How it Sounds if Your Kid Writes it

Here is the view from the seat of an admissions officer:

In a cyber security competition club, where knowledge and leadership are critical, officers used the club for personal gain by hoarding crucial information. Focusing only on their success, they ignored the remaining thirty members, leaving us without proper guidance. When I became Vice-President, I began addressing this very important issue. I appointed officers with all the appropriate leadership skills to ensure the club functioned per its written Constitution. To raise the overall skill level of the club, I arranged weekly knowledge share sessions, which were not only informative but also fun. Additionally, I held monthly one-on-one conferences with each team to ensure their ideas were heard and that the members all felt included in the process. With these changes made, all five teams qualified for the California Platinum Finals, for the first time ever in the club's history.

This might appear in Rudransh's autobiography, but is it the best page? Is it the page you would tear out and keep if you were on the Pacific Crest Trail and had to jettison weight?

Sounds like a good kid, but the admissions officer doesn't read any further. This paragraph could be replaced with other paragraphs I've read from other students, which means it doesn't qualify as a paragraph no one else could write.

It's not Rudransh's fault. Students are asked to write about challenges they faced and extracurriculars where they made significant contributions. As it sounds now, however, we learn less about Rudransh than the club. And it could be any club.

Rudransh needs to find what matters *to* him, not what matters *about* him.

An English teacher might start with the verbs. As it stands, he *began addressing, appointed officers, arranged sessions,* and *held conferences.* Sounds like he's idling in middle management.

But stylistic advice is not that helpful. It's hard to say, "Rudransh, can't you just jazz this up with more active verbs?" The jazzy version uses oddly strong words to describe a tepid situation:

1) "began addressing" becomes *spearheaded*
2) "appointed officers" becomes *recruited*
3) "arranged sessions" becomes *coordinated*
4) "held conferences" becomes *hosted*

We feel like we've streamlined, word smithed, and emboldened. But now he sounds like a middle manager with a good editor. Perhaps he's applying for a promotion.

This is where a lot of advice falls short. An uninspired writing style is not a sign that Rudransh is an uninspired writer. It's a clue that something else is wrong. Rudransh doesn't need to say things differently; he needs to see writing the essay as an entirely different job. What should we ask?

Questions for facts are liberating because they have concrete answers.

1) *What moment with your club made you most angry?*
2) *What one person joined the club because of your leadership?*
3) *Which competition will you always remember and why?*

Whatever answers arrive are not really open for debate. Facts are facts. The answer to question 2 is blessedly concrete: Henry. The first human in the essay.

Henry was from engineering rather than computer science, and his insight led to an uncommon victory. Henry is a fact that helps us learn that Rudransh built a better team by opening the ranks of a CS club to non-CS people.

This story doesn't end up in the final cut because Rudransh decides it's more about Henry. (Perhaps it was the essay that got Henry in?) But it illustrates the power of fact-questions.

The next questions seek a different kind of fact known as a thought. Thoughts are facts, too, because just like Henry they do exist. They are a little harder to pin down than Henry because thoughts are facts that live in the mind. They require explanation.

"It was raining" is a fact that doesn't require explanation. "I think it was raining" is a thought that prompts us to ask why. (Why are thoughts still facts? Because whether it rained or not, it remains a fact that you think it did.)

Here are the thoughts I seek from Rudransh:

4) *What idea from your sessions changed the club the most?*
5) *How did you know your club's Constitution was any good?*
6) *Why is inclusivity a priority for you as vice-president?*

Fact-questions need only your memory to report; thought-questions require your mind to explain. The answer to question 4:

> *One question from a novice forced me to go into the smallest deepest parts of an operating system, where I first understood what an operating system actually was. This made me a better teacher.*

Some students write an entire essay just to build up to such a moment. Rudransh is thinking aloud about what he loves and why, but decides it isn't that different from what most people learn when they teach. He keeps it for a supplement.

Beyond facts and thoughts is a third kind of question I call an elephant. Elephants can't be answered by recalling a fact or explaining a thought. They require reasoning. They often call the whole essay into question.

> 7) *Is inclusion really more important than talent?*
>
> 8) *Why is cyber security so important—isn't CS all about open sources like GitHub?*
>
> 9) *Why is hoarding information so bad—isn't it the aim of security to keep information private?*

Everything, if we look closely, contains contradiction. Contradictions in the essay are not flaws that threaten to damage it. Finding a fundamental contradiction gives us something to ponder, explore, and resolve. If you're lucky enough to find it, don't sweep it under the rug!

Facts and thoughts tell who, what, where, and when. But an elephant finds the why. Elephants are always there, but students work hard to avoid them rather than beating the bushes to flush them out.

Elephants make us want to read more. If provoked an elephant might disrupt the story you think you're telling so you can tell it better. The most important thing about an elephant is that it requires Rudransh.

I asked two questions about inclusion:

6) *Why is inclusivity a priority for you as VP?*
7) *Is inclusion really more important than talent?*

The first is a thought-question that led him to explain the value of interdisciplinary problem-solving. The second is an elephant that forces him into new territory: *nobody argues against inclusion!*

Discovering an elephant might require a moment of Devil's Advocate. Devil's Advocate is a form of questioning that adopts an unpopular position to test the strength of its opposite. For example, the atheist Christopher Hitchens was asked by the Pope to argue against the beatification of Mother Theresa. Hitchens argues that she is a terrible person. This allows the Church to entertain the best arguments against her before proceeding to beatify.

Getting too good at playing Devil's Advocate is intellectually dangerous, because flipping things upside-down can confuse us about things that matter. Which is of course the Devil's hope. The only thing more dangerous than being good at Devil's Advocate, however, is being bad at it.

This is because Devil's Advocate invites deeper understanding. If we ignore our mental defense against the Devil, our conclusions remain unexamined and we look lazy. To earn command of our opinions, we must give the Devil his due:

"Rudransh, why do you think it's such a good idea to include less talented people in a club whose aim is to win a competition?"

Silence.

If I asked this upon meeting Rudransh, I'd either be a jerk or an oversized debate nerd. But at minute forty, a lot of water has flowed over the dam. I have earned the moment to knock him off-balance.

His response is understandably defensive: "I am from India but live in Sacramento, so I have spent a lot of time feeling alienated."

Notice his answer is not about the club. It might be considered wildly off-topic. It is also not obvious: knowing what it's like to be an outsider is not a straightforward reason to be inclusive. For some people the experience of alienation gives reason to shut the door once you're inside.

His response is terrific news. He is not saying something he thinks he is supposed to. My blunt question drew out the elephant hiding in tall grass, and in just one sentence Rudransh says something more personal and honest than anything in his original essay.

Rudransh writes about what it's like to be Indian in Sacramento. There are some upsetting instances of racism and some happy moments of friendship. This material is raw and honest but still might describe many people in many cities. This doesn't mean we scrap it for something new. It means we keep talking.

I try flipping the question.

"Have you ever been to India?"

Hearing about life as an Indian in Sacramento, I cannot help but wonder how it compares to life as a Californian in India. He nods and thinks and talks:

"The funny thing is I also feel alienated there."
"How so?"
"My grandmother lives in Chennai, and I think of that place as an extension of my own home."
"But alienating?"
"It can be."
"What's it like when you visit Chennai?"
"It's very crowded."

His eyes shift focus from me to some imaginary point in the distance over my shoulder. He's picturing Chennai. Then it all comes pouring out, and I scramble to write down every word:

> *One of the things I remember clearly is after a long time they finally built a basketball court near my grandma's house and that was important to me. Mostly they are playing cricket on the court which defeats the purpose. But that was something that kind of confused me: did they not want to learn a new sport or cricket was just so important? I don't know if it's true or not, but I heard that people in the community were unwilling to play basketball on the new court and even wanted to destroy it so that they had more space to play cricket. It was a very crowded area where hundreds of people were playing multiple games of cricket all over the place with no regard for others. One of the most important experiences specifically was when I brought a basketball to play and people asked me to leave. A man watching this happen came over to me and explained how he wanted to play basketball, too, but the same thing happened to him. This was when I heard about the idea of destroying the court. I couldn't understand the reason people were motivated to do this.*

This agitated ramble is marvelous. Rudransh is discussing something important to him. How can we tell? He says so in the first sentence: *that was important to me*. Why does he pause to tell me?

I see this all the time. He's apologizing for saying what he wants while giving himself permission to say it. It's as if to say, "Bear with me, I know this sounds odd, but this is important." Whatever comes after that is guaranteed to go in the essay.

It's also fun. Shall we turn the screw once more?

"Rudransh, why is it so important for cricketers in Chennai to learn basketball? Aren't you just swapping one sport of empire for another sport from another empire?"

"Basketball is an amazing sport. People in India are good at cricket, but I've never heard about star basketball players or programs in the country. They must be building a court so people with talent in that area could shine. It's important to have a more diverse skill set. Cricket is not in the Olympics. I was hoping- there was an instance where kids were playing basketball and because of my Tamil language I was easily able to communicate with the kids and help them understand the game and play my favorite sport with others. They had no concept of the double-dribble."

Plenty of people have made their school club more inclusive, but do you know anyone who converted cricketers to basketball in Chennai? Rudransh is speaking from the heart, and what he says is specific enough to be irreplaceable.

How did we help him find it? Not by pivoting away from his boring cybersecurity club, but by taking a closer look at it.

His essay toggles between being a better ambassador for basketball in Chennai and building a better cybersecurity club in Sacramento. These two experiences rely on similar skills and insights, but the crux is something he didn't know in advance of our discussion: being an outsider in one scenario makes him a better insider in another.

Cliché? Genius? Doesn't matter—it's just what happened. If you think it sounds good, that's because it's true. If you think it sounds silly, then too bad, because it's true. Carnegie Mellon recognized the real thing.

In Chennai, speaking Tamil helps Rudransh shift basketball's image and relate to the kids who want to play it. In Sacramento, he learns that a strong crop of freshmen is important to the success of the club. Deepening the bench creates a club that people want to join.

We also finally understand why Rudransh is so committed to the club's Constitution. In Chennai good rules about the

64

use of public facilities prevent grief. He cares about the rules because the right rules make institutions better.

Conversation in this chapter was more intense than stuff we've seen so far. Finding the elephant, playing the Devil, poking the hornet's nest. I said before that my biggest asset in this process is my ignorance of your kid. My second biggest asset is my willingness to provoke.

As a parent you've now seen how to skirt pitfalls, ask good questions, and listen well. Pushback is different. It's saying, "Not so fast." If you have secretly wanted to do this all along, there's good reason: it's fun. But instead of arguing in a way that prevents the essay, now you can argue in a way that improves it.

Arguing shows the complexity of your kid's thoughts from the inside. When you play Devil's Advocate you are speaking on behalf of thoughts, rather on behalf of yourself. You are in one sense starting and then listening in on an argument between your kid and herself.

Here are some questions that force scrutiny:

But I thought you said x?
How could that be?
What does this have to do with that?
Could you make the opposite case?

I hope it's clear that pushback is not judgment. It's a form of respect that deepens our intellectual relationship with kids. It gives them power to argue intelligently back.

Pushback is both personal and impersonal. It's personal because these are real events and thoughts from Rudransh's life. It's impersonal because they deserve scrutiny no matter whose they are.

Pushback-questions are only effective once your kid has gone far enough down a path to know what she thinks about something. Not perfect knowledge, just a perch from which to be reflective. It's hard to be accountable to one's thoughts without first becoming familiar with them.

Most college essays make claims that sound respectable but avoid what one truly thinks, which we only discover when pressed. Students wear the cloak of social justice, for example, because they have learned those opinions are safe.

Nope: *I labored tirelessly to make our club more inclusive because it's the right thing to do.*

Nope: *If we start to look beyond superficial things that define us then we grow as a community.*

These truisms go unnoticed as part of the white noise of our cultural moment, however true. Unreflective claims are strategically bad for two reasons: they sound hollow, and they don't help us get to know you. Also people don't like to be told the obvious.

Yup: *Did making our club more inclusive mean we would lose the competition? Probably.*

Yup: *Including Henry would be awkward if he felt the need to speak for all engineers.*

Just like your kid, people who turn up in his essay are complex and not replaceable by the thing one might hope they illustrate.

Experts on the essay say you need the courage of your convictions, as if once you have an opinion, you must ride it to the end of the track. I say instead that you should be *accountable to your opinions.* Speaking from the heart takes courage but also builds courage.

If as a parent you are too good at Devil's Advocate, you might find yourself having changed your kid's mind too easily. Don't let him off the hook with a mere change of mind.

If Rudransh had said, "Yeah, I guess you're right, talent probably is more important than inclusion," then I would need to play Devil's Advocate to my own Devil's Advocate and say, "Are you sure? What about Henry? Or what about the double-dribblers in Chennai?" My aim is for Rudransh to grapple with what he thinks.

"Changing your mind" also shouldn't be just another Holy Grail. An over-leveraged epiphany is melodramatic. To work, it must be true. The truth is a labyrinth, and the best essays enter because they need to.

JOHN DEWIS

Part 3 - FREEDOMS

JOHN DEWIS

7. The Opposite of Boring

If you ask your kid, "Any thoughts on what you might write your essay about?" and she says, "I think maybe coding," the corners of your mouth might turn down a little. You might say, "Isn't there a place to list your intended major?"

At this point in the book, you know a question like that about the essay is verboten. Once you start asking the right questions, however, does the essay always come surging out on a river of tears and with a flourish of trumpets?

No, sometimes it takes time. This chapter is about patience. Have faith. Steer the course. Things are boring until they aren't.

When I ask Jennifer if she had to spend all day every day in one class in school, which one it would be, her answer arrives before I can finish the question: coding! I'm eager to learn why.

"What do you like most about coding?"

Silence. That's a good sign. It means she has to think. Then, the answer:

"I don't know."

More great news! If she doesn't know yet, this conversation will be interesting, and she'll be done in an hour.

I have learned that this Zen optimism can be counterintuitive for parents. You might think, "Coding is coding, what can you say about it?" And then her own *I don't know* verifies your hunch. You suggest a different topic.

I know your help is well-meaning, but here's the unlucky road you have accidentally sent her down: coding is never discussed again, and Jennifer writes an essay that starts with counting chin-ups, gritting her teeth, and wiping sweat from her brow because she thinks she might as well tell how a small but hard-working kid has become a pretty good cross-country runner, and it will show her perseverance.

In which case she's viewing her life from the outside for the benefit of the essay, rather than through her own eyes for the benefit of herself. Learning things about herself will help admissions get to know her. With the sweaty chin-ups, they won't read past the first paragraph because they don't need to. They've read this one before.

As her parent, you have the power to return her to her rightful position behind her own eyes. It's not time for a fresh horse. It's time for specific questions:

"Which is your favorite coding language?"
"I guess Java. And Python."
"If you had to spend all day coding in Java or Python, which would it be?"

We laugh at the thought that I'm only capable of asking where she would like to spend the rest of her life. Jennifer thinks about it.

"Well Python has intricacies that I don't like. Java basically has– is explicit. You have to write everything to make it work, but Python is implicit– you have to– it doesn't have variable types. In Java you have to declare exactly which type of variable it is, but in Python when you make a variable it assumes a type depending on what you tell that variable to be doing."

I'm including this part of the conversation for a reason. Many parents think:

This is way too technical for the college essay!
I have no idea what she's talking about, and she doesn't either!
Oh my God it's a foreign language—no one in admissions will get it!
This isn't about my daughter, it's about coding!
Honestly, it's boring!

In fact, it's perfect. Don't stop her!

First, she hasn't answered my question about why she likes coding. She's done something better: compare two coding languages.

Second, she's in her own zone talking from herself as herself and possibly even to herself. She is not in the land of the college essay or its topics, which means she's not struggling to demonstrate anything. One good clue is that her phrasing is so choppy I'm not even sure how to punctuate it.

Third, she's trying to figure something out. The great Russian theater director Stanislavsky said there's nothing more fascinating to watch than a child untangle knots in a string. We are watching Jennifer untangle her thoughts.

She writes for ten minutes about coding. Because I don't know what she's talking about, I ask questions appropriate to my ignorance:

"What's an example of a variable?"

"In programming you can have Cup objects that are all Containers but... not sure how to explain this. You can kind of have Cups and Bowls, and both are Containers, but not all Containers are Bowls and not all Containers are Cups."

"And Python and Java deal differently with these things?"

"I guess I'm looking for things that are similar and have similar functions so I can connect the two ideas."

Most sessions that yield a great college essay after just one hour include the phrase, *I'm not sure how to explain this.* That's no coincidence.

Seeking to explain something is one great justification for writing at all. This writing also tends to be clear because it has to be. Explanation is an exercise in making the unclear clear. The struggle draws us in, and we find ourselves in good company and rooting for you. Untangling knots is the kind of writing that helps us get to know you.

It might look like the shift from boredom to confusion is a downgrade. You might think she should be looking for something exciting or heartwarming. Confusion is actually a great thing to discover.

I'm delighted when a student raises her hand in class and says, "I'm confused." Students usually think this is a big wrench thrown in the machine and terribly awkward news to the teacher who is supposed to be making things clear. On the contrary, if there isn't enough confusion in the classroom, I wonder whether students are being challenged. I model comfort with confusion by saying things like, "I wonder why that is" or "How wonderfully confusing."

Aristotle goes even further and says confusion is requisite for epiphany. Perplexity precedes insight. For Einstein, mass and energy look incommensurable until the moment they are interchangeable. Using Aristotle and Einstein to help make my point must mean I'm worried it does not yet speak for itself!

What Jennifer writes next still doesn't end up in the essay. But it is the necessary bridge to it. The perplexity before the insight. Well-meaning parents will worry she's off-track, and so will Jennifer, if you let her. When in fact she's on the verge of the essay that gets her in.

My one-word questions to Jennifer appear in square parentheses:

"In Java there is less guessing when you go to debug, which is inevitable, so having those types declared is more useful, because then you know the flow of the code. [Flow?] When fixing specific errors, like when a function receives a variable, it's impossible to mess up on the type of object it receives. It won't compile if the function expects something and you give it something else. [Compile?] For variables in Python, the code itself does not know what it is and might do something with it, but that something might not work. An array for example is a list of things, and in Java everything in an array has to be the same type. [Array?]"

If you resist the urge to judge it, the train of thought keeps running. If you say, "Let's not get too technical," then you've kicked the train off the track. How can I be so sure?

"This is amazing stuff for me to be learning right now. Thanks for your patience in explaining it to a non-CS guy, Jennifer."

"Sure!"

"I have to admit parts of it are hard for me to grasp. Does our own spoken language suffer any of the same glitches of coding languages?"

She thinks. "I don't speak any Cantonese and my grandma speaks no English, so conversation is always an approximation."

Like a bolt of lightning, Jennifer just wrote her first sentence. All the better that she doesn't realize it.

"Like when?"

"I forgot how to say the word 'cup' and so I asked in Cantonese for 'the thing you drink water with but not a water bottle.' In this case she brought me a bowl."

Jennifer just wrote her second sentence. In the best of cases, my own work is done. Do you agree that she has stumbled from a tangle of coding into a clear statement of personal significance?

How did it work?

First, I never judged anything she said. I only asked for clarification. Always more, not less. I kept the foot on the pedal.

Second, I really listened. I never paused and said, "I think what you said is great, but can you make it more accessible to the reader?" The reader for now is just me, a human with whom she happens to be in conversation. If it needs to be more accessible, I ask a question that requires a more accessible answer.

Third, the material she used to explain coding inevitably came from outside the world of coding. You might be tempted to congratulate her for devising the perfect metaphor for coding: talking to her Taiwanese grandmother. But that's not how it worked. Jennifer needed Grandma to explain herself.

If we had started our session brainstorming instead of talking, then her grandma would have appeared on a list of potential topics. If I asked her what she likes most about her grandma, she would have mentioned a Cantonese dish that her grandma cooks. And her college essay would have begun by describing the smell of something Grandma cooks, its name italicized in Pinyin, and the essay would have illustrated the point that if your grandma comes from another country, she probably cooks something delicious from that country.

That's the essay Jennifer would have written, and if she got into Stanford, it would have been despite her essay rather than because of it.

The smell of cooking we love and associate with our roots is powerful, but it is also the most common way to demonstrate appreciation for our immigrant experiences. The experience of becoming a better coder by talking to Grandma in so-so Cantonese is special to Jennifer. It's why Stanford liked her.

I'm going to point out one more thing that appears almost miraculous, until you see the logic that makes it ordinary. The example she found to explain why she likes coding is precisely the example she offers later in a non-coding context: cups and bowls. Did you notice that and think it was strange?

The essay was already hiding there. She hadn't programmed anything in Java using cups and bowls; but when forced to talk about Java, she was already sourcing the intellectual challenge of living in a bilingual house. She had already chosen Grandma.

I shouldn't assume you think this is a promising essay yet. But it is. Luckily there are details in her opening that warrant further explanation. That means the essay gets to keep going, confusion being the right weather for epiphany.

I don't even need to ask the next question, which might have been something like, "How does it happen that you live with your grandma from Taiwan?" She's already writing it:

> *My parents moved here as teenagers from China; they speak Mandarin, Cantonese, and English, and often translate for us. I took Mandarin 1 and 2 in high school but I'm actually more interested in learning Cantonese because it's a dialect and not the official language. Going around in China, Mandarin is more useful, but in Chinatown SF everyone pretty much speaks Cantonese, and the language has a diverse food culture- and I kind of want to be able to order beef noodle soup (or get a cup from my grandma) without asking my parents.*

Second paragraph done. Then she writes for a bit about Chinatown, food, and her own experience in China. It's all interesting stuff, and all hers, and lives in our shared document, but it doesn't end up in her final 650 words.

When she stops, I ask her the question I'm still pondering, since it's how she started this whole thing: "But what about programming?"

> *Unlike Cantonese and English, programming has perfect rules for translating- there's a defined way that the user writes to change between objects. For example, because Rectangle and Square objects both have positions, widths, and heights, you can write your own function to make a Rectangle from a Square, through copying the Rectangle's attributes. Of course, this doesn't work for everything. Just like a Rectangle can never become a Circle, some words in Cantonese just don't translate into English: min directly translates to "face," but its attributes (the things that define it) are totally different. It's a term central to Chinese culture, meaning "the feeling of being respected and honored by others." Min dictates almost every interaction between Chinese people, who strive to "save face." You never open gifts when the giver is there, for example, and disagreements are saved for private moments.*

Third paragraph done. "But, still, does this help you program?"

> *I think my sensitivity to ambiguity in language makes me appreciate Robotics more than other coders on my team, where I get to see a lot of my programming in action.*

Nice! Sounds like the first sentence of her fourth paragraph.

Notice that we are marching through another college essay genre: My Robotics Competition. If we'd started there, Jennifer would have been prompted to write a genre-specific essay about how she loves to tinker and how she tinkered her way through a robotics victory, and she would be indistinguishable from the herd.

Just like Grandma, the robotics competition is only told in service of her own actual investigation of language. Here's where it goes:

> *This was the first time we made it to the national championships in ten years. It was an interesting game this year based on adequate placement. The robots had to cover "rocket bays" with pizza-sized circular pieces of polycarbonate (with Velcro on their edges). The task is focused on accuracy. It's fun to watch robots that aren't that accurate because they tend to slam into walls randomly. As a programmer on the team, I work with a vision system to align with the targets. The Boeing 737 struggled because its system often steers the plane, which means the pilot might fight the AI.*
>
> *What happens on the practice field doesn't always translate in a match. Our vision system shines light off of reflective tape on the field to identify the rocket bays. To test our system, we used a wooden practice field. The actual field, however, had aluminum railings, and we found the reflection of our lights would come off the target but also the aluminum bar behind it, so we had problems tracking the target properly. We had no idea how to fix it.*
>
> *We tried both eliminating one of the LEDs and making the lights less bright by covering them with electric tape, but that made it hard to find the targets at all. My solution was to filter out those targets that included the aluminum reflections. The invalid targets were skewed by 60 degrees in either direction, so we filtered that data out. It worked.*
>
> *One lesson here is that you have to test things in realistic conditions. There is an idea in programming called test-driven development where you write a bunch of tests that your code should pass and find the one it breaks, find out why, and fix it. You might think it's*

safe to assume that if it works most of the time it will work all of the time, but there's always an "edge" case that your code breaks on. When it comes to my Cantonese, I could test-drive by literally flying to Hong Kong and see where I mess up. But the real test would be how well I can talk with my grandma.

What's the lesson for parents? Resist temptation to redirect conversation.

Does that much technical detail help them get to know you?
Will admissions be familiar with Java or alienated by it?
Is your college essay about Chinatown?
Isn't highlighting ethnicity a bad strategy for Asian applicants?
How about we brainstorm and see if anything else speaks to you?"
Shall we put together an outline?

What's truly helpful is a conversation where you ask questions to find out more, where you don't think about the essay, and where you help your kid get back to being herself rather than demonstrating something about herself.

What's truly helpful in this case is patience. Do not allow your boredom or her confusion to be an obstacle to epiphany. Let what is most interesting to your kid lead her.

She hits plenty of essay topics if she wants them: growing up bilingual, my robotics competition, my grandma. They work because they weren't plucked from a brainstorm or thought of as topics. She needs them to explain herself. Jennifer shows how honest thinking can defy genre and dissolve cliché.

Allow her to simmer in confusion, knowing it is the perfect weather for lightning. If you're confused, too, that's a good thing. It means you don't have to search long or work hard to ask real questions.

8. The Opposite of Lonely

One of my best teachers in college wasn't in the classroom. Iris and her husband worked the ranch out at Deep Springs College. She used to ask us to do all kinds of stuff we didn't know how to do:

Well, walk the whole pipeline then until you find the leak.
I said stand in the gate on your horse and don't let anything by!
Put that uterus back in the heifer and hold it until we sew her up.

I didn't imagine at my Quaker prep school near Philadelphia that these would be things said to me in my freshman year of college. But I'm glad they were.

Years later I asked Iris where her confidence came from. People trusted her and did what she said. She thought for a second and said matter-of-factly, "I never asked you to do anything I wasn't willing to do myself."

I used to ask my fellow English teachers when they last wrote a five-page paper on *The Great Gatsby*. Usually, thirty years ago! But how many had they assigned? Thousands. If you're an English teacher, try it. Better yet, ask your students to grade it.

Parents, you know what's coming. When was the last time you wrote a 650-word essay about yourself? Probably when you applied to college. This might be true even if you are a best-selling author. Why not try it? It won't be lonely because you know someone else doing the same thing. Why not sit down and write together?

It's such a simple idea, but almost no one does it. Parents are often completely taken aback by the suggestion. As if nothing could be more unnatural than to write next to someone with whom you speak every day and to whom you might have read aloud every night for the first years you knew each other.

There is a writing taboo here rooted in cultural norms. Perhaps also in our very conception of personal identity. When you write for yourself or about yourself, we think it must be by yourself. We think it belongs in a locked diary, under your breath, or behind closed eyes, like a prayer.

Social media has certainly challenged this norm, broadcasting thoughts that would have been considered private a generation ago. On Twitter people communicate instantaneously to millions without thinking twice. If we can do it for 55 words, why not 650? What happens to our writing once we think of it as writing?

Before the days of Zoom I drove around Los Angeles and sat at dining room tables with high school juniors, and we would write together. It was the best job in the world. I have such happy memories of those days. My first student got into Harvard despite mediocre grades, and after that I never advertised. I just got phone calls from anxious parents who got my number from so-and-so.

I lived in Venice and scheduled my afternoons from east to west so that I ended the day at home. I started in Larchmont with a student or two right when they finished school. Then I would make my way west: a student in Laurel Canyon, one in Beverly Hills, one in the Palisades. Then an ocean swim in time for the sunset if I was lucky, and a late dinner at the Golden Bull on the Pacific Coast Highway. I tucked my cash in the ashtray of a car so cheap no one would bother to break into it, a butter yellow 1982 Mercedes 240D.

It felt strange to sit there watching someone else write. An unfair dynamic skewed the writing; since I was the hired expert, students were focused on pleasing me or sounding smart, and they ignored their own burning questions. The assumption of my expertise was counterproductive.

I am happy to elicit someone's thoughts, but I can't pretend to be an authority on them. Not anymore than they could be of mine. So, I took out a pad and pen and started writing alongside my students. I found myself asking questions and then saying, "You write what you think and maybe I'll write what I think, too." This was a little shocking to some students, for whom writing had never been social.

Most writing we do in school, and therefore our entire youth, is done alone. You sit at your computer in solitary confinement and try to say something smart. Then you carefully pass it to an adult, who reads it alone, judges it, writes on it, and passes it back to its author, who retreats to the shadows to digest the verdict.

Students and I developed a very different rhythm, and writing took on a different purpose. For one, it gave me the chance to write. Which I liked. I wrote about horses I'd known, my best friend's divorce, mountain lions, my family, students, chess. I discovered I was not writing to persuade or even to communicate, but to think and to find out. It was freeing. And a sixteen-year-old is a great audience: discerning, honest, imaginative, quick to laugh.

More to the point, my students' writing went through the roof. This was true whether or not I ever shared what I was writing. Just the company helped, I think. And the lack of rules. If I did share what I wrote, and it contained sentence fragments because that's how it came out, then students were emboldened to let their own thoughts arrive unadorned, too.

Students and I also learned most questions don't have final answers. It helps if I'm taking a stab at the same thing as the student. And if we both share what we write, it becomes obvious that although we are together, we are wandering different rivers. *What do you think?* or *Why did that happen?* is a much better atmosphere for discovery than *Have you convinced your reader yet?* or *But where's your evidence?*

The most common reaction from a student reading aloud what she wrote was always: *You mean I can just write that?* To which I always reply: *But isn't that what you just wrote?* It's a joy to see students impress themselves with their own honesty. Writing quickly, easily, and from the heart builds confidence for moments when it gets harder. What could be more accessible than our own current thoughts? I learned that writing need not be the product of thought; it is thought itself.

Writing "separately together" is especially useful for the college essay. When the material is nothing less than oneself, it's clear her work cannot be mine or mine hers. Our uncompromising singularity primes writing about ourselves to be a good shared activity.

This is less straightforward with other aims of writing. If a student and I are writing alongside one another about a poem by Sylvia Plath, and if she needs to hand in a paper on the poem, there is a risk that a lazy or crafty student might borrow something from me unattributed. There are plenty of ways to prevent this. One is to stick to Devil's Advocate and only adopt positions that the student opposes. Another is to avoid reading your own work if you think it contains groundbreaking analysis.

I remember one day at a student's house up on Mulholland Drive. When I got to my seat at the big table there was an envelope. Connie sat in her seat and said, "My mother wants you to read my report card." I opened the envelope. "Oh, that's actually my sister's," she said. "But it's okay—they're the same."

I said, "Why don't you write that down."

"That I'm the same as my sister?"

"Sure, if that's something interesting to write down."

"My sister is a senior, and I'm a junior."

"Why don't you write that down. And then write down this half-sentence and keep writing: 'The thing most similar about my sister and me is…'"

She looked at me like I was crazy, which prompted me to say, "And I have a sister, too, so I'll write down the same thing and then keep writing."

She wrote for fifteen minutes without stopping, so I did, too. I didn't know what she wrote, but the way she wrote it had the look of sheer honesty: fast, furious, focused, and unfussy. I figured we better keep going.

"How about now we use a different start: 'The biggest difference between my sister and me is…'"

Another fifteen minutes. When she paused she saw me scribbling away. When I paused I saw her scribbling away. The sound of pens on paper is good company when you're not sitting an exam.

"Should we find out what we think about our sisters?"

We took turns reading our work aloud, paragraph by paragraph. My sister has little to do with hers, but we both have sisters. (Actually, I have two, and I wrote about both.) We came up with questions for each other we wanted answered most.

What did your sister ever do that made you most mad?
What did you do that made your sister most mad?
What about your sister do you most admire?
What about you does your sister most admire?

Then we answered them. She laughed, she cried, and she wrote. Our hour together was almost up. I asked Connie to read through her work and underline every sentence she thought was good.

What was the test? If it was something I could not have written about my own sister! The thought was whatever she writes shouldn't be replaceable. Otherwise, admissions might replace her.

Then I asked her something I was curious about: "What will you do differently next year when your sister goes off to college?" I left her to answer this alone at her living room table and let myself out.

The next week when I turned up at the table, Connie read me her essay. I recognized the material as the very words that poured out of her at the same time last week. Great first sentence, too:

> *If I accidentally showed you my sister's report card it would be okay because it's the same as mine.*

I don't have a copy of her essay, because I never read it anywhere but at the big table. But I know she got into her first choice, Northwestern, same as her sister.

This was an epiphany for me: how to write your college essay in one hour. I shifted my tactics. The goal was not to write well; it was to generate honest material quickly and without fuss. Students clocked in at 1500 to 2000 words an hour.

The challenge was cutting it down to the best 650, but the relief was that the best 650 were already there and didn't need to be crafted from the void. My average number of sessions with students went from ten starting junior year to two anytime at all before fall admission deadlines senior year. If two meetings did the job, I could work with many more students.

First Skype and then Zoom took my travels online. I found that meeting over a Google doc worked even better than at the table. I could write my questions on the same page where the student could think aloud.

When people make referrals, they start with the people they care about most: relatives. My next generation of students were far from Los Angeles: Houston, Seattle, New York, London, and Shanghai. My business was remote ten years before the pandemic. I got phone calls from people I'd never met: *You helped my neighbor's cousin get into Princeton; do you have time to meet with me?*

I accidentally built a college admissions consultancy by putting a simple question into practice while I wrote alongside students: What if the best purpose of writing is not to communicate what we think but instead to figure out what we think?

I had a student last year who woke up in the middle of the night and rambled a voice-to-text response to something we'd wondered about during the previous day's Zoom. She put it in a Google doc and it became almost word-for-word the essay that got her into both Harvard and Yale. (Now she needs a late-night ramble to help her decide where to go.)

I was always taught that writing was re-writing. But here I was discovering that writing was pre-writing. How do I explain a phenomenon where the easier the process the more successful the product? Some possible answers:

1) Writing is not the product of prior thinking but a form of thinking itself

2) A good way to produce writing is just to write down whatever you're thinking

3) Thinking without a plan produces perfectly coherent and compelling writing

4) Writing that is just thinking aloud might perfectly communicate what matters

I started thinking of writing as a technology rather than a skill. Technologies are tools designed to help us achieve goals regardless of skill. And often the same technology can be used to achieve different goals. The same blender can make a banana smoothie for breakfast, homemade mayonnaise for lunch, and a mushroom bisque for dinner. Writing can be an email to a colleague, a blog of Harry Potter fanfiction, instructions on a post-it for how to water my trees, a sonnet with a quill pen, or my name scratched on the beach with a stick.

Thinking about writing as a technology helps students put it in its place. We are not at the mercy of writing. The basic function of the writing technology is to externalize thought via marks on some surface like paper or a computer screen. We can write whatever we want.

Thinking about writing as a technology helps prevent us from fretting about whether we are any good at it. Getting good at writing might not be anything like, for example, getting good at playing baseball. Baseball is a skill not a technology. You don't use baseball to accomplish something else. The purpose of writing, on the other hand, doesn't need to be to make a good piece of it. In the case of the college essay, the purpose of writing is just to help someone get to know you. The writing technology (like a blender) doesn't require a talent for it, just access to it. You don't ever ask someone how good they are at using a blender.

Thinking of writing as a technology makes a lot of conventional conversation about the college essay incoherent. For instance, "Did she write a good college essay?" not only seeks unhelpful judgment but also misunderstands the technology. It would be like asking, "Did she do a good job using the cup to get water to her lips?"

For most, writing is a process whereby we groom prior thoughts for an audience. Which means we see it as an account of what thought produced rather than an account of the thinking. If writing is just a technology for externalizing thought, however, then "writing well" is available for anyone with thoughts.

For this reason, you will not hear me say things like, "Well he's full of great thoughts but too bad he can't write well." It would only ever have to be something like, "He's full of great thoughts but never took the trouble to write them down." This would describe many students whose expertly polished essays do not correspond to their actual thoughts. It's possible to write clearly without saying anything.

In case it's hard to get beyond thinking of writing as a communication skill, here are some underappreciated uses of writing as a thinking technology:

1) Allowing one's thoughts to become known to oneself
2) Asking and answering one's own burning questions
3) Generating thoughts new to oneself
4) Revealing thought's hidden logic by putting it on paper

If we see writing as thinking, then we can ask freshly whether writing also succeeds in making those thoughts accessible to others.

At this point in the chapter, we've seen two tactics that might seem at odds: writing side-by-side (writing socially) and getting your thoughts on paper without any thought to the audience (writing your mind). I hope it's not complicated to imagine these two things working together. When I write side-by-side students, I am not the audience for the student's writing. Sometimes we listen to each other, but we are not writing for each other.

And there's no pressure to share, either. The process is social but what's written is not. This is because the goal is not firstly to communicate your thoughts, it's to think them.

Students are usually surprised when haphazard writing arrives fully equipped with its own logic. We shouldn't really be any more surprised by this than that a haphazard baby arrives knowing how to drink milk. Thoughts might be the very expression of logic rather than something that requires it. In the way that a baby, despite all evident frailties, is the very expression of practical survival.

Lest we get too dizzy thinking about thoughts, let me offer a takeaway that I hope gives you confidence to let your kid ramble all the way to Yale: if thought arrives with its own logic, then written thought is probably organized enough.

You might think the virtue of planning ahead is to provide a blueprint, scaffolding, or a skeleton to be fleshed out. This makes it sound like the essay is a building or a body. Are those reasonable comparisons? Are we going to live in the essay for ten years like a house or for our whole lives like our body, or is someone just going to read it for 90 seconds?

It's true that a human being can't stand up without bones. But I might remind you that a human is not built skeleton-first and then enhanced by whipping up a bunch of other stuff around it.

These structural aspirations are counterproductive for writing the essay that gets you in. People like to say in response to this: *You don't have to follow the outline, but you better have one!* I disagree with this on the grounds that the outline is hard not to follow once you have it. And it puts you in an odd relationship with yourself where you establish rules just so you have something to break.

Part of the virtue of an outline, I presume, is that once you've made point A you are free to move onto point B. But as we've seen with many wonderful runaway trains of thought, what happens between A and B is precisely what matters and is precisely what's missing in the essay that followed the outline.

People are sometimes afraid just plain old thinking will be rambling and chaotic. Not so sure. Thinking is disciplined, in my experience, and sometimes we must work against that discipline for the pleasure of surprising ourselves.

These people also say: *Sure, go ahead and create a splat sheet where you get all the raw stuff out, but then you've got to go back and put it in an outline, edit, re-edit, and polish.* I say nonsense. Sounds time-consuming. You're not assembling a Boeing 747. You're letting someone into your mind. It takes about as much time as turning on a light.

Of course, you don't just magically have full access to your mind all at once. You need a way in. The best way is to hop on a road and take it there. Any road. For more than one quiet student on Zoom, I have asked about the painting behind them on the wall, and what they said next was the essay.

"What's that on the wall behind you?... Oh, interesting. How about you write that down, and I'll write about the painting on the wall behind me."

This is how I have written a stack of unique essays on *Penn's Treaty with the Indians* by Benjamin West. Writing together provides traction and a reason to stay on whatever road you've found.

Let's think back to Connie at the big table up on Mulholland. *What do you like least about your sister?* makes us laugh and results in a bit of writing. *What do you like best about yourself?* is not an outrageous question to follow, although it would have been forced if it had been the first question.

You might find yourself sharing something about your own thoughts that you never shared before or thinking something you've never thought before. If you've never written a paragraph about your sister, then whatever you write is going to be something you've never written.

You might be surprised if you hired me to work with your kid and discovered in our shared document a paragraph about my two-year-old son's favorite Simon-and-Garfunkel song. But if you read what your own son wrote at the same time up at the top of the page, you would appreciate the exercise.

"What's your favorite song?" prompted him to write about a riff he developed on the opening chords of James Taylor's *Fire and Rain*. And somehow it led him to write about how he changed his stroke technique as a rower and helped his school win nationals, and to marvel at the way machines depend on rhythm. He thinks music will make him a good engineer. I challenge any naysayers to develop an outline for this essay and convince us that he could have used it to get into Princeton.

I am not applying anywhere, so my own writing is just there, doing nothing in the universe except existing. But it's useful to see how thoughts can be valuable and cheap at the same time. Because they come from us, they are dear to us.

Because they come to us incessantly, like waves on the beach, they're also cheap.

Students are often looking for their Holy Grail essay. They think there is a big difference between a great thought and just any thought, and so they dismiss the stream of thoughts they live in. This is a damaging relationship for a young person to have with thinking. It's like turning off the tap to go look for a drink of water.

My point: Try writing side-by-side with your kid.

I'm picturing my friend's father painting next to me in the field from the *Introduction* to this book. And then instead I'm imagining my friend and his father painting next to each other in the field. That might have been a memory they would have forever. It might have resulted in paintings they would have forever. And there's no question it would have resulted in different paintings.

I'm surprised we don't spend more time writing with each other, given that we spend a big part of our lives sending emails to each other. Why don't we use it to get to know each other? Or to find out what we think? You can.

9. The Opposite of Writing

For each request from a parent, I get ten from kids. They read their own work and think:

Why does my life sound so generic?
Why do I have nothing interesting to say?
Why does this essay sound like an algorithm?

They realize something is wrong. They realize some strange force is at work on them. And they are in great company. How is it that students almost universally struggle to say what happened, what they think, or what they care about?

Because they've never done it. Whether we know it or not, most of us have been trained to think of writing as an exercise in formal rhetoric. Most high school students can tell you how to construct a five-paragraph argument deploying Aristotle's three tools of persuasion: ethos, pathos, and logos. Most can tell you what a thesis is and how evidence helps prove it. I don't claim to know what the job of writing is, but I don't have any reason to think five paragraphs in support of a claim is a great instance of it.

Not many of us have ever been given a writing assignment to tell a simple true story, figure out what we think, or tell someone what we care about most. Since those are things that help another human get to know us, we are underprepared for the exercise, should anyone ask. Then college admissions asks.

If we think writing is the formal presentation of an answer plus the research that led us to it, then no wonder the college essay is a fraught enterprise. It must seem like you are being asked to have a thesis about yourself. And not just any thesis, *the* thesis.

"Thesis" comes from the ancient Greek verb meaning *to place*. It could be something simple, humble, and low stakes: putting something on the table for a closer look, an opening parry, an idle thought, a wonder, a dare, something to test out, try on for size, or take for a walk.

The first thing that happens to a thesis in Hegelian philosophy is that it collides with its antithesis. Hegel was a long-winded German philosopher who wrote at the start of the nineteenth century. For Hegel the collision of thesis and antithesis, and their resolution in a new synthesis, is the inevitable and eternal movement of all thought, which always follows the same fate. It's great training in not being too attached to your thesis. Your thesis was born to die.

Students and parents are typically aligned in thinking that whatever else the essay is, it had better be the perfect encapsulation of the contents of your heart said in a way that stands up against the scrutiny of all the world who will use it to judge you for all time. Without reassurance from Hegel, it might be really upsetting to imagine such an essay on fire by the side of the road.

We've already seen how it might be better to think of writing the college essay as texting a bunch to yourself. Or tweeting to a small audience. Or you when you are just being yourself. Daydreaming?

We don't usually spend time outlining a text before sending it or worrying too much that it will fail to capture our essence. And yet, why is a text so coherent? It contains a thought, reaction, insight, plan, or question. And it's dashed off in the way short important things get to be. Let this be a clue to how easy writing can be.

Other ways of asking the question of this chapter:

How has an entire generation come to think of writing as an elaborate trick?
How best to free your kid from its grasp?
Why do college essays sound so wrong?

If you had to concoct a recipe for trickery it might be this: convince an unknown powerful panel of judges of the validity of an airtight thesis about your own talent and depth of character in a brief, poignant, highly polished writing sample.

For young people, writing is a test. It's how to prove they know something, read something, or can follow directions. In many cases writing is nothing more than a demonstration that they are capable of writing. All the better if the content itself doesn't matter. Writing in school is sometimes the intellectual equivalent of digging a hole to fill it.

Or as my father likes to say, when given the chance,

"Your mother just talked to me on the phone for a whole hour."

"Oh, about what?"

"She never said!"

When the SAT added the essay portion it seemed like a nod to the human taking the test. What they must have found, however, was that if they give a vague prompt and then assess how well responses follow a published format, students produce 50,000 generic essays.

This is what it's like for admissions, too. It's why the University of Chicago asks questions like what it might be like to be a butterfly, and why Stanford has a section for fifty-word responses to questions about what music you like, where you would time-travel, and to write a letter to your future roommate. And why Deep Springs College wants applicants to tell when they were asked to do something mundane, frustrating, or physically exhausting, and to describe your chief intellectual virtue and vice.

The SAT went the other way because it didn't want to judge things it wasn't entitled to, like what you think it'd be like to be a butterfly. Instead of asking for original content, they now ask students to critique an already existing essay, like a speech by Jimmy Carter. What does it mean if writing about what someone else wrote is considered a better object for assessment than an original essay about something you think?

The College Board, who makes the test, wants to assess something called critical thinking skills. How do they grade it? You judge Jimmy Carter's mechanics, logic, evidence, and ability to persuade. And then they judge how well you judged Jimmy. To be fair this task is closely aligned with what students often do in high school. But it is even more closely aligned with something else: what teachers often do in high school.

Educators talk about the importance of modeling behavior: young people mimic the adults around them. If adults in school are, above all, assessors, then it seems inevitable that the skill cultivated in the young will be assessment. And the SAT has now confirmed it without a shred of irony: they are assessing student assessments.

What if the skill we wished to model were something better, like thinking? Observing? Devising? Making art? Building something? Changing your mind? Being kind?

I'm not suggesting the SAT be in the business of assessing those things. But I am suggesting that writing as an activity has been bankrupted by the need to demonstrate mastery. Schools are missing one of our best chances to think better, take risks, know ourselves, and care about others. Lots of schools have missions that include these aims, but few see writing as a way to achieve them.

96

Then, against the backdrop of an educational system that has demoted writing to a clerical exercise, the college essay appears out of nowhere. An old idea persists because college admissions actually cares about the content. They care what you think. They are not judging whether you have successfully internalized the writing format. They want to know if there's anything left once the format is gone. They want to know if you have survived the experience.

Often the answer is no. Because our essays in school deploy evidence to support a thesis, most college essays do the same. We feel like we are being played because we are.

I'm hoping this will show how resilient I am.
I'm hoping to make them see how much I care about other people.
I'm hoping this illustrates that I'm really smart but also really funny.

Imagine how excited admissions is when they get an honest 598-word essay about fixing the headlight on a Pontiac Fiero.

Your kid just accomplished something that eludes the grading rubric of the SAT and his high school English class. He just made someone smile. He just rescued someone dying of boredom at the admissions table.

The point: writing is not only not what we've been taught; it might be the opposite of what we've been taught.

Kevin had written all kinds of stuff about makerspace competitions, school science awards, coding, robotics, Elon Musk. He's very into this stuff, but so are a lot of kids. One question found Kevin:

"What's the coolest thing you've ever built?"
"My Pontiac Fiero."

He describes it in great detail. We don't want a description of the car someone would get from googling it. We want it to be unmistakably Kevin.

Are these the questions you would ask?

"When was the very first time you ever saw a Pontiac Fiero?"

"In New Jersey when I was twelve."

Another fact under our belt. Let's look for a feeling.

"How did you know you loved it?"

"I didn't. I didn't think, 'That looks cool' so much as 'What is that?!'

You know the rest. He devoted most of his essay to something he jerry-rigged to fix the pop-up headlamps. It's the opposite of writing as Kevin used to know it, because it just tumbles out, because he is not giving a single thought to style, because he doesn't care how he might appear to be, because he is unabashedly telling us about something he loves.

The essay itself is a complete afterthought. It's something that gets written because he's busy not writing it. Kevin is just talking about when he fell in love with a car. He doesn't transport us to his garage by talking about what it smells like, which is what a college essay workshop might convince you is a grand idea.

Nonetheless, you can anticipate parental skepticism about the Fiero:

1) *What if no one on admissions likes old cars?*
2) *But that car is the least impressive thing he's engineered!*
3) *Isn't it a little too much car and not enough Kevin?*

My responses:

1) *Doesn't matter if they like cars—he's made us love a Fiero.*
2) *Plenty impressive—he MacGyvered the headlamp with a paperclip!*

3) A zealous descent down the rabbit hole is a great way to get to know someone.

These things result in a great portrait of Kevin, which is an odd claim for me to make, considering I've only spent two Zoom-hours of my life with him. Which is one hour 58 minutes and 30 seconds more than he'll get with admissions.

I've included my comments so you can see what I look for when I'm helping a student fine-tune. He took some comments and ignored others, which is perfect. He's in the driver's seat.

Apart from the unapologetic obsession and crackling prose, the best thing about this essay is that he pulls it off with 52 words to spare.

When I was twelve, I saw a Pontiac Fiero on a street in New Jersey while on vacation. I didn't think, "That looks cool" so much as "What is that?!" The thing that attracted me to it was its mysterious appearance - what *is* that thing, how many were made, what makes it special? If I see a Honda Accord driving down the road, it looks routine; but if I see a car from the 40s, I don't know what it is, and I instantly become curious and want to find out more. I was so captivated by this Fiero that as soon as I got home, I researched everything about it. What I discovered probably should've turned me away, but I just fell more in love. Manufactured briefly in the mid-1980's, Fieros are notoriously underpowered and suffer from engine fire issues. Ignoring these trivial problems, I quickly grew to love this little underdog of a car for its quirks like pop-up headlights, a mid-engine setup (the engine is behind you to help with handling), and a fiberglass body that won't rust.

When I turned fifteen, I saved up, bought one, and set about fixing it up. Those fun pop-up headlights turned out to be real devils, since I twice had to take them out and rebuild the motors that power them. The torque pins that hold the gear in place had turned to dust in the thirty years since the car was built. I thought replacing the pins with new ones would be simple, and it should have been, but I mistakenly pulled out the center of the motor assembly too far and had to spend the next hour and a half building my own tool to fix my mistake. A paper clip wrapped around a staple turned out to be the MacGyver-like solution I needed. I held one end of the paper clip and used the other end, along with the "hook" of the staple, and grabbed a little pin out of the way to slide the motor assembly back in. Success! However, when it came time to put the headlight back together, I overtightened the motor housing and cracked the gears, so out they came again. I put new gears in right next to my new torque pins, and the headlights now pop up and down without a hitch! Through trial and error, I grew more skilled at repairs over the next couple years and tackled bigger projects: the clutch, bumper, engine gaskets, and radiator hoses. At this point you might think my dream car sounds more like a nightmare, but that's part of the allure to me. As crazy as it may sound, I love that my Fiero breaks down from time to time, because it gives me new challenges and stamps my car with a certain uniqueness.

With the big Fiero jobs behind me I thought, "What next?" Last summer, I built a small motorcycle from old bikes, a lawnmower engine, and scrap metal. Yes, I could've simply bought a motorcycle, but the challenge of designing and creating a minibike was what I really enjoyed. Every time some little issue presented itself, like the chain continuously falling off, I grinned and started thinking of ways I could fix it. It might not be pretty, but it came from my own hands and hard work; that makes it infinitely better than anything new from a store. I take pride in my projects, and I'm looking forward to bringing this same passion for designing, building and fixing things to the Formula SAE team in college.

John Dewis
This is a great opening paragraph- we can tell you love the car and against some better judgment. It's strange in a good way, too. I would say that as you edit this down further you will be able to tighten this paragraph- for instance, you say at least four times that you love the car (attracted, captivated, love, love). You might strengthen our sense of your love for the car by reducing the number to the moment or two that really got you.

John Dewis
I suggest deleting "this meddling kid" because it plays into a feature of many essays (not your fault- the fault of the genre), where kids sometimes take on the view of themselves as if an adult is judging them. In your own mind, you are probably not a meddling kid- in fact you are restoring the car, which requires meddling. If you are aiming to say something from the standpoint of the car, that is different, and you might find a way.

John Dewis
This is the most provocative idea of the essay for me as a reader: a car that breaks down is better than a car that doesn't. Really? Anyone who has loved something like this understands, and most people will relate. What is it, I wonder, that makes the car unique in this case? Is it stamped with something of you? Your time? Your thoughts? Not sure. Whenever I see the word unique it is a good sign that you could replace it with the thing that makes it unique. Another sentence after this one might do it.

John Dewis
Why? Have you stopped driving it? Has it stopped breaking down? Hope not. Ha!

John Dewis
Continuous means without ceasing (like the seasons) whereas continual means happening again and again. I think the latter is the one here but not 100% sure.

John Dewis
Not sure- a bit like "that meddling kid!"

John Dewis
I think you should explain why your own is better than from the store. Not easy to explain perhaps but worth it.

Parents might say: "Holy moly, you better slap a conclusion on this baby about how engineering has restructured your mind to problem-solve beyond the garage and how you want to tinker away all the big problems facing humanity!"

To which I say: "Nope, they'll be delighted by a short essay. They've already put it in the 'yes' pile—why give them reason to second-guess it?"

Kevin got into his first choice, Dartmouth, and everywhere else he applied, too. I got a nice email from his mom a year later:

> *John,*
>
> *Thanks so much for your help! A fun anecdote from the admitted student visit at Dartmouth:*
> *I was walking to a parent session and they had admissions folks lined up pointing the way. I happened to notice and recognize the name of the woman that had written a personal note that accompanied Kevin's letter of acceptance. I went up to her and asked if she was in charge of the PNW region and she said yes and asked where my student was from. I said Seattle and then clarified _____ High School. (At this point she didn't know my name or [Kevin]'s name and [Kevin] wasn't with me and there were several applicants from _____ this year).*
> *She LIT up and exclaimed, "The car kid's mom!!" and then waved to her colleagues and said, "It's the car kid's mom!" In a sea of tens of thousands of applications, they remembered the kid from Seattle because of his passion for automobiles and I'm sure, that essay about fixing the headlight on his Fiero. It was amazing and reaffirming that the essays (and our kids' passions) really do matter!*
> *Thanks so much for helping Kevin figure out what his essay needed to be about and giving him the tools to craft an excellent piece that reflected his voice and who he truly is. He really enjoyed his discussions with you,*

and you made the prospect of essay writing not quite as daunting.

Sara

This email supports my hunch that the essay must be specific enough to be irreplaceable, and that real details matter.

His mom thinks the magic to my method was knowing what the essay needed to be about. As you know now, I never had any idea what Kevin's essay needed to be about. I just let him talk. When it came time to sift through a couple thousand words, the stuff that couldn't have been written by anyone else might have felt like strangely TMI on the car stuff. This is what made him famous in Dartmouth admissions as the car guy.

Would it have worked if he'd written, "Let me tell you something right now: I'm a car guy." Nope. How about if he got all twisted up about how working on cars has taught him patience, commitment, and problem-solving, with a careful example of each? I think not. It was about how he used a paperclip to fix the flip headlights on his Fiero.

Conclusion – Make your help help

Parents are typically happy to outsource help on the college essay. But sometimes, just off-screen, I see a stray arm. Or before a student answers a question, her eyes dart to the side and back.

At which point I always say,

"Oh hi! Is that your mom? Hi Mom! Why don't you join us?"

Thinking you might need to hide is a symptom of how problematic this process has become. I don't think you should hide.

If a kid loves the fact that her mom is there but didn't realize it was okay, then we've just cleared the air. If she hates that her mom is there, now Mom must reckon with her. It's a win either way.

As parents you have been made to feel unfairly nervous about tampering with the essay. Sometimes demystifying the college essay is just reminding you there are no rules. Your kid does not need to be kept in a hermetic container to avoid skewing the data. She need not be stored in a cool dry place. She's just thinking about how to spend the next four years.

What if she were leaning on her elbow on the front lawn pondering a spear of summer grass? If you went over and lay on the grass somewhere nearby, do you think the college essay police are going to jump out from behind a tree and warn you that her thoughts are confidential? Just ask her if she wants to be alone and she'll tell you.

As a parent you've been a major part of the journey of this young person. I feel bad when I see concern about contamination now, as if sixteen years of parental guidance must arbitrarily stop when it comes to college admissions. I appreciate the impulse to be respectful of her independence. As you've seen in this book, however, if you are open and curious about your role, you can liberate the process in unexpected ways—for both of you.

Alia

For instance, if Mom says something interesting, I might say to the student,

"Why not write that down."

The student looks at me in horror and says, "But my *mom* said that."

And I say, "Yes, why not write that down."

And she writes down: *My mom says x.*

And I say, "At first you were reluctant to write that. Is it because you disagree?"

And she says, "Yes, I think y is more like it."

And I say, "Why not write that down."

And she writes down: *But I think y is more like it.*

Usually, these two sentences go straight into the essay:

> *My mom says until a treatment is approved it's not right to offer it to patients, even if they sign a*

waiver that says they understand the risk. I think people should be able to make those decisions for themselves in matters of life-or-death.

Alia's mom is a VP at a large pharmaceutical company. She had the authority to pre-approve the one-time use of a potentially lifesaving treatment. Mom decided not to honor the request. Sometimes risk of harm is greater than potential help.

Alia is interested in public health. She's trying to figure out whether she holds her mother responsible for someone's death half-way across the globe.

This makes an engaging essay because it explores an actual dilemma for her mom and complicated feelings for Alia. Alia describes her journey through medical ethics prompted by a dinner-table argument.

I'm not suggesting you need to appear in your kid's essay. Usually not. But there's no rule about it. If it helps Alia chase down an answer to her burning question, or find her question in the first place, then go for it. It was just lucky that Alia had a conversation with Mom that grabbed her and set her moving.

Alia is not using Mom to improve her essay but to help understand her own moral compass. They're different people. In the throes of investigation, we tend to go anywhere we need and grab anything that might help.

In most cases parents do not magically catalyze the essay. But I still like roping you into conversation. Happily including parents in an investigation can help maintain our focus on a question rather than perfecting an essay.

How someone deals with a live question creates a great portrait, because answering a question evolves at the pace of thought. It is free to engage the thoughts of others. This freedom requires a cognitive reorientation away from the essay, whatever it might become, and towards present thoughts, whatever they might be.

Trying to answer a true (typically unanswerable) question is also simply a chance to talk openly about something with your kid. Or wonder about something collectively. I've come to realize this collective wonder is rare. And I've also come to realize why.

Conversation between a parent and a kid is usually "about" the kid. Not about what he thinks, but about how he's doing. About your kid in an administrative or therapeutic sense.

What if the conversation were about anything else? Medical ethics? Something from today's news cycle? Or the headlight on his Fiero? Shifting focus off your kid takes the burden of brilliance off him and the burden of expertise off you.

This shift has been useful for me in the classroom, too, far away from the land of the college essay. And it's the key to a truly inclusive classroom, which might include someone walking by the door at the wrong time.

Once it included a kid's mom who called while he was in class. Instead of sending the kid to the office for having his phone on, I had him answer it and ask his mom whether it was okay for Antigone to break the law against burying traitors in order to bury her brother.

Mom helped me domesticate an otherwise rarefied practice of literary interpretation for a room of ninth graders. Her answer was that the state is not supposed to interfere with religious practice. It sent us down a provocative line of inquiry. Why do I care what Mom thinks if I'm not grading Mom? Mom is not an object of assessment. Neither are you! We are trying to figure out how to judge Antigone's crime. We need all the help we can get. It also meant I already knew someone at Parents' Night.

Another time while teaching in this same ninth-grade English class, the classroom felt a little crowded. I counted the kids: twenty. I asked the class, "Aren't we eighteen in here?" It turns out we'd had two extra kids in our class all week. They had an un-proctored study hall that period and heard freshman English was where things were happening. One of them handed in an essay on Somerset Maugham's *Razor's Edge*. I couldn't believe it.

One of the virtues of having what I call "the third thing in the room" (not you and not me) is that we can throw our focus onto something that isn't any of us. So much so that I didn't particularly mind who was there. This has a magical way of enlisting our thinking and promoting our listening rather than feeling the need to claim knowledge or stake territory.

This setting makes the source of thought less relevant than the thought itself. And it makes the reasons for the thought more interesting than the rightness or wrongness of the thought. It helps people find the music in themselves rather than looking for themselves in the music.

What I'm describing is an egalitarian impulse with respect to thinking. Who you are affects your opinion, but it doesn't change its value. This climate dissolves whatever power dynamic might otherwise get in the way. When parents and kids talk like this with each other, they are equals in the eyes of thought.

I hope as parents you will feel licensed to be more useful conversationalists, rather than worrying if your help is too little or too much. I hope you will see that the type of help is more important than its degree. You don't need to be a silent partner, distant administrator, or anxious lurker.

Aditi

Dad is sitting half offscreen as his son and I talk. Aditi reads from the essay he's pasted into our shared document. I ask him to read the first sentence of the second paragraph aloud:

"Epistemologically speaking, I know that there are certain undercurrents that result in forms of communication that one would consider lackadaisical, but on the other hand people have come to expect a certain modicum of decency when it comes to basic human interaction."

I turn to Dad and ask, "Does that sound like your son?" They both crack up.

"Aditi, would you please explain what you are saying? A second ago you were talking about your name, and then it went all epistemological."

"I was just trying to say that I can forgive people for mispronouncing it, but not after I've corrected them."

"Can you write that down?

And so on. Rather than feeding the madness, Dad helps me expose the college essay conspiracy. A conspiracy that temporarily robbed him of his son. Together and with good humor we help Aditi see that unless he says what he means, he renders himself unrecognizable to Dad and incomprehensible to admissions.

Aditi's essay is his exploration of his own name and why it matters to him. He tells the story of running for school president, where all he did onstage in front of the school was provide instructions for how to pronounce his name. He got elected. It's a lot of fun, and only he could have written it.

Why can't Dad be in the room? He doesn't have to be, but he can be. Dad is the guy who named him.

Chella

Mom overheard her daughter laughing all the way from the other side of the house and decided to see what was going on. Half a torso enters stage left.

"Oh, perfect timing! Chella, is it okay if we ask your mom? Chella was wondering if saying 'sitting is the new smoking' is okay or if it risks offending any smokers who happen to sit on admissions… or for that matter, sitters!"

An interesting conversation followed. Mom is cautious but enjoys weighing in. Notice I didn't ask her something she wasn't entitled to know, like:

"Mom, do you think it's relevant for Chella to write about her talent for playing the *viol da gamba,* or would that go better in a supplement?"

If I did, turn my bad question into a real one:

"I have no idea. Chella, what do you like most about the *viol da gamba?* What's your favorite piece of music to play on it? Why?"

In the meantime, the "smoking" question is a fair third object in the room for us to wonder about. It's not about Chella, it's about etiquette.

"Well, Chella, you've heard what two oldsters in the room think. Hope we haven't taken you off-track."

Chella keeps it. In part because she gets another sentence to explain what she means by it. She designed and built a chair for the front hall of her house with a forward sloping seat. It's a place for putting on your shoes but not for lounging. She wanted to know if it was possible to make a chair that was useful but discouraged sitting. Interesting!

Her original essay was written under the influence of the college essay. She talked a lot about the importance of design without ever mentioning anything she designed. Her new essay was her written response to a few pointed questions: it was genuinely about her, what she makes, and what she wants to make next.

Chella's mom wrote me a nice email saying she couldn't believe what she'd overheard and was grateful that I took care in getting to know her daughter, who was accepted with a nice scholarship to NYU.

Mom was always open and interested in what her daughter was thinking and writing but aware of the risks of helping. Since she ended up laughing along with us for a few sessions, I asked Mom for her perspective on why this process worked so well. I told her I was writing a guide for parents.

This is what she wrote:

John,

You made Chella feel like she was perfect the way she was. Your insisting that she portray herself as she is came through so powerfully in her essay. The website of a college help service organization we had secured help from, showed off a before and after essay. To me the before essay looked much better than the after one. The after one made the essay so flowery and generic, it lost the writer in the process.

Your approach to the common app essay where Chella was not forced to answer one of the seven common app questions (open format) gave the freedom to Chella to express what meant most to her about herself instead of restricting her to answer one of the seven predefined questions. Just as in court, they say not to ask leading questions, answering a question may taint the answer with the question itself. But without a person like you, it is extremely intimidating for a 17-year-old to tackle.

When you talked to Chella for the Common App essay, I felt like you were a psychologist. Your listening ability was excellent. You had her pause at the right times to elaborate, expand, or clarify what she was saying.

You showed a genuine interest in her work which made her open up and talk about her work without any hesitation. Your curiosity (which would also be the curiosity of the reader) took her from answering one question to another which eventually formed the essay. So, in fact, we can say, that the essay is actually your interview of her with your questions being in the background of the reader's mind as they read through her essay.

Your general knowledge (Pythagoras, Plato, Shaker Furniture, and Frank Gehry) gave you the ability to contrast who she was with others to draw her image more sharply. For example, you mentioned another furniture designer [Sam Maloof] who did not use math at all when he made furniture.

Your own command of the English language, grammar, vocabulary, and style helped Chella give shape to some of the thoughts she had a hard time expressing. One of the many pieces of advice you gave her was 'Start the sentence with you or what you are discussing as the subject' to make the sentence active.

Your calm, pleasant, and non-judgmental demeanor put Chella at ease in talking to you. You always encouraged her to go on her line of thought and never said "This won't be good," or "Do you have something else to talk about." You were down to earth and easy to connect with, which I feel is of utmost importance.

Thank you,
Sowma

I am of course flattered by this testimonial, but I'm including it because it's a list of accessible tactics for parents. Together they create a portrait of careful listening. Sowma also reveals so much about what many parents value.

Notice that Mom's description of the process contains no tension between my help and her daughter's honesty. Holding Chella accountable to the things she says begins by taking the time to notice them. And that can be you.

As you've seen here and in *Hack the College Essay,* the mere freedom to speak for herself doesn't guarantee that she will. For one, she may not know how. Good listening guides you to good questions. And good questions free her to discover what she thinks. That is the freedom we are after.

Once she finds herself in the presence of her own honest thoughts, however, there's a lot less freedom than we might think. Now she must deal with her thoughts. She's on the hook. That's the essay.

Certain things will demand her attention over other things. These are almost always the same things that demand ours. If she discovers convictions, they will have her courage, because she'll recognize them as her own.

If she discovers a lack of conviction, she will feel accountable to explain that, too, because she will see that it matters. If she discovers confusion, then she will have your good company and will discover that confusion is good weather for epiphany.

Mom is right: Chella is perfect the way she is. So is your kid. That's how I know whatever comes out will be the perfect essay. Which only sounds crazy to anyone who hasn't read the *Parent Guide.*

Her next question is likely to be: "You mean I can just say that?"

And your answer: "But isn't that what you just said?"

Appendix A - Pointers

• Observations from the trench that just might help.

A conversation is collaborative, even if the essay itself is not.

If you let your kid be irreplaceable, which she is, it's difficult for admissions to say no.

To put it simply: people are not topics.

Expert advice and parental fear have conspired to prevent Jake from writing his essay.

They are actual questions that have arisen in my effort to hear and understand Jake.

The trail into his mind cannot start where it ends.

The things that matter will turn up because they must, rather than because you said so.

Don't look for evidence that your kid is blemished or shiny, just evidence of your kid.

Non-judgment is not wishy-washy; it is a highly disciplined form of investigation that lets a kid think what he thinks and spend time figuring out why.

You should never write under the influence of the college essay, because it will end up sounding like a college essay.

Instead of asking your kid to demonstrate something, ask him to figure something out.

He thought it sounded deep, and a combination of expert advice and parental restraint helped him think he had succeeded.

If the essay is bullshit, it doesn't need you or me to say so. It will stink when we get close to it. So that is exactly what we do.

Students usually choose something that sounds uncomfortable over something that is uncomfortable.

Mental discomfort enjoys an infinite landscape of possibility, and if you get specific enough you can find your very own.

"Go through your document from the top and highlight in some color of your choice whatever you think is the most necessary or most true material."

Notice how too much explanation ends up being more efficient: in the old version it took him 150 words to get to his million-dollar idea; in the new version it takes just 50.

If we see how his mind was working, we have a better chance of sympathizing.

I'm making sure they have a chance to sit with discomfort long enough to discover its effect on them.

Otherwise, we jump over the discomfort to celebrate the lesson, overlooking the reason the lesson is a lesson in the first place.

I can appreciate the wish to reveal what your kid is not willing to reveal about himself. But oneself cannot easily be revealed by another.

Each impulse to answer turns into an impulse to listen.

This is why good questions are better than good topics.

You don't want your kid to be an example of a certain kind of kid, you want her to be herself and stand only for herself.

I was about to say, "Why not write about math—you love math!" but then I thought to myself, "You seem to be really good at math, but do you love it?"

We can see now that a Why-not-talk-about-x question is a just sneaky variation of an If-I-were-you assertion.

The reason to write it down is not to put it in your essay. The essay gets discovered after a series of true, personal, or interesting things get written down.

My objection, apart from that this paragraph was written by someone other than Noah, is that making it conversational just makes it strange.

Just using the phrase *the core of who I am* does not mean we get to know you.

With only ninety seconds to tell us who you are, you don't want "distressed" to be what we remember.

The thing that unites these things is the thing we care most about: Tati.

Don't we think and talk in ways that grab what we need when we need it? We don't say, "Hey that's off-limits, can't you tell this conversation is about asteroids?"

Rudransh needs to find what matters <u>to</u> him, not what matters <u>about</u> him.

Rudransh doesn't need to say things differently; he needs to see writing the essay as an entirely different job.

Finding a fundamental contradiction gives us something to ponder, explore, and resolve.

The only thing more dangerous than being good at Devil's Advocate is being bad at it.

He's apologizing for talking about something he wants to while giving himself permission. It's as if to say, "Bear with me, I know this sounds odd, but this is important." Whatever comes after that is guaranteed to go in the essay.

Rudransh is speaking from the heart, and what he says is specific enough to be irreplaceable.

If you think it sounds good, that's because it's true. If you think it sounds silly, then too bad, because it's true.

Since in the above process you are speaking on behalf of thoughts, rather on behalf of yourself, you are just starting and then listening in on an argument between your kid and herself.

Sadly, she is viewing her life from the outside for the benefit of the essay, rather than through her own eyes for the benefit of herself.

Learning things about herself will help admissions get to know her.

One clue she's onto something good is her phrasing is so choppy I'm not sure how to punctuate it.

Most sessions that yield a great college essay after just one hour include the phrase *I'm not sure how to explain this.*

First, I never judged anything she said. I only asked for clarification.

If it needs to be more accessible, I ask a question that requires a more accessible answer.

Do not allow your boredom or her confusion to be an obstacle to epiphany.

When you write for yourself or about yourself, we think (wrongly) it must be by yourself.

The assumption of my expertise was counterproductive.

I learned that writing did not need to be the product of thought; it was thought itself.

I didn't know what she wrote, but the way she wrote it had the look of sheer honesty: fast, furious, focused, and unfussy.

What if the best purpose of writing is not to communicate what we think but instead to figure out what we think?

I don't claim to know what the job of writing is, but I don't have any reasons to think five paragraphs in support of a claim is a great instance of it.

Writing as an activity has been bankrupted by the need to demonstrate mastery.

The essay itself is a complete afterthought. It's something that gets written because he's busy not writing it.

As you know, I never had any idea what Kevin's essay needed to be about. I just let him talk.

It reaffirms our focus on a question-at-hand, rather than on perfecting an essay.

Talking about something random takes the burden of brilliance off your kid and the burden of expertise off you.

Egalitarianism with respect to thinking makes the source of thought less relevant than the thought itself. And it makes the reasons for the thought more interesting than the rightness or wrongness of the thought.

Appendix B - Rules

• *Hack the College Essay* gives one rule per chapter. The *Parent Guide* gives rules whenever we find them so I've compiled them here in one place.

Practical reasons to help your kid with the essay:

1) Helping your kid is moral
2) Most parents want to help their kids
3) Most parents end up helping anyway

Four Rules of Engagement.

1) Be ignorant
2) Be specific
3) Don't be judgy
4) Don't mention the essay

The "Instead of" Rules:

1) Instead of trying to think of topics, try to ask good questions.
2) Instead of worrying about the suitability of a topic, just say yes.
3) Instead of getting her to demonstrate, get her to investigate.
4) Instead of trying to "show not tell" try to "think not show."
5) Instead of calling bullshit, just get close to it and we will notice its smell.
6) Instead of saying that you did something, say what you did.
7) Instead of saying that you think something, say what you think.
8) Instead of saying that you realized something, just say what you realized.
9) Instead of courage of her convictions, think accountability to her thoughts.

Writing rules:

1) Explain what you actually did in the necessary level of detail.
2) Cut a first paragraph if the story is clear without it.
3) Let things happen in the order they happened.
4) Prioritize the challenges and solutions that changed you most.
5) Describe your current self in ways that make you proud.
6) Distinguish carefully between past and present thoughts.

Nopes and Yups, set 1:

Nope: ---> Yup:
Urgency --->   Curiosity
Expertise ---> Interest
Feedback ---> Inquiry
Answers ---> Listening
Wisdom ---> Presence

Nopes and Yups, set 2:

Nope: ---> Yup:
Supervise ---> Unearth
Suggest ---> Provoke
Control ---> Free
Govern ---> Unleash
Manage ---> Observe

Nopes and Yups, set 3:

Nope:
You should think about writing your essay about that.
That sounds like a great topic to brainstorm.
This observation could make a great conclusion.
If I were you, I would absolutely run with that.

Yup:
Can you write that down, what you just said?

Rule of Superlatives:

To elicit maniacal specificity ask questions with superlatives:

first time,
last time,
most fun,
most true,

most wrong,
most different,
most surprising,
favorite,
funniest,
scariest,
worst,
hardest,
least,
highest,
best.

Prohibitions and the rules we made from them:

1) No false subtlety ---> 1) Make real comparisons
2) No false psychology ---> 2) Be concrete
3) No false sincerity   ---> 3) Be sincere
4) No symbolic feelings ---> 4) Find your actual feeling
5) No figurative language ---> 5) Phrase things directly

Reminders about confusion and discomfort:

1) Don't hide from confusion, look for it. I model confusion by saying things like, "I wonder why that is" or "How wonderfully confusing."
2) Don't hide from discomfort, look for it. When you extract feelings from facts, make sure they are the feelings that matter, not just the comfortable ones.
3) Don't confuse discomfort with drama. Rocky montages (beads of sweat, chin-ups, hearing a voice say to keep going) are too universal to be yours.
4) Specific mental discomfort explained in detail has a good chance of being specific to your kid and will help us get to know her.
5) Confusion is good weather for epiphany, but don't let your kid replace herself with an epiphany or dramatize it.

6) "I don't know quite how to explain this" and "Saying this will destroy the whole point of my essay" are statements that precede writing the essay that gets your kid in.

Reminders that challenge what many think:

1) The essay itself is not the aim, it's an afterthought.
2) Do not translate your kid's writing into an essay format.
3) Neither micromanage nor macro-manage.
4) Don't replace idiosyncratic facts with big lessons.
5) Don't choose social justice truisms you think sound good.
6) Trust that your kid reconciles many disparate parts.

Three kinds of questions:

1) "Fact-questions" seek just the facts which are non-negotiable.
2) "Thought-questions" require figuring out what you think and why.
3) "Elephant-questions" disrupt claims, discover contradiction, and can require Devil's Advocate.

Writing without the need to communicate:

1) Writing is not the product of thinking but a form of thinking.
2) A good way to write is to write down whatever you're thinking.
3) Writing without a plan can produce coherent and compelling writing.
4) Writing that is just thinking aloud might communicate what matters.

Some uses of writing for yourself:

1) Allowing one's thoughts to become known to oneself
2) Asking and trying to answer one's own burning questions

3) Generating thoughts to oneself

4) Revealing thinking's hidden logic by providing a record of it

Points of clarification:

1) Conversation has no fixed rules.

2) Conversation is collaborative.

3) You can ask your kid about things other than herself.

4) You can ask your kid if she wants to be alone or have company.

5) Real investigations grab at anything or anyone that might help.

6) Two people writing about the same thing will write different things.

Sowma's List:

1) Your child is perfect the way she is.

2) Your child can come as she is and be who she is.

3) Your child is replaced in most essay workshops by something flowery and generic.

4) Your child is free to ignore the prompts offered by the Common App.

5) Your child is free to say what matters most to her.

6) Your child should not be asked leading questions.

7) Your child can be listened to excellently by you.

8) Your child can be asked to pause at the right time to elaborate, expand, or clarify.

9) Your child and her work are of genuine interest.

10) Your child will be open-minded if you are.

11) Your child writes the essay by answering good questions.

12) Your child writes the essay by participating in a real or imaginary interview.

13) Your child writes the essay by letting real questions live in the mind of the reader.

14) Your child will draw her image more sharply in company with your own knowledge.
15) Your child can be called on her assumptions.
16) Your child can shape her thoughts with basic command of English.
17) Your child can make herself the subject of her sentences.
18) Your child will be at ease if her company is calm, pleasant, and non-judgmental.
19) Your child can follow her own line where it goes.
20) Your child is easy to talk with if you are down to earth and have a sense of humor.

Appendix C - Myths

• Much of my advice goes against conventional wisdom. Read these nuggets of bad advice and bad questions to avoid them, but please do <u>not</u> mistake them for rules!

This is really her job and the best thing I can do is stay out of it
I need to remember that this has nothing to do with me
It's a rite of passage and she's just going to have to figure it out
I'll edit your final draft for grammar
I'll make sure you weren't shy about putting your best foot forward
I'll make sure you didn't forget to show what a kind person you are
Video games are too scary; why not write about something similar but different?
Why not write about your childhood before video games were part of your life?
Instead of video games, can you try writing about the divorce, move, and dad?
Remember at scout camp when you were afraid to scale the wall but then did it?

Remember how hard you worked to win the science prize with your Tesla coil?

Remember in soccer when you nursed your ACL tear back in time to win States?

I think this makes you sound dishonest

But I remember a lot of great stuff my kid has probably forgotten!

But she refuses to share all the best things about herself!

But this is the one thing she's never been able to do!

But my kid's writing is totally in the clouds!

But I know my kid better than a lot of people!

But I know my kid better than he knows himself!

Why not write about math?

But you are so good at math, and you love it!

As a person who likes math,

As a stressed-out junior starting BC Calc,

As someone for whom math just always came easily,

It doesn't sound like me, but is it better?

Isn't there a separate place where you can list your intended major?

I think what you said is great, but can you make it more accessible to the reader?

Does an essay requiring that much technical detail help them get to know you?

Will most people on admissions be familiar with Java or alienated by it?

Is your college essay about Chinatown?

How about we do a little brainstorming and see if anything else speaks to you?"

Shall we put together an outline?

Have you convinced your reader yet?

But where's your evidence?

Did she write a good college essay?

Is she a good writer?

Was she good at using the cup to get water to her lips?

I'm hoping this will show how resilient I am

I'm hoping this will make them see how much I care about other people

I'm hoping this will illustrate that I'm really smart but also really funny

What if no one on admissions likes old cars?

But that car is the least impressive thing he's engineered!

Isn't it a little too much car and not enough Kevin?
Holy Moly, you better slap a conclusion on this baby!
Holy Moly, you better say how you want to tinker away big problems facing humanity!
Let me tell you something right now: I'm a car guy
Mom, does playing the viol da gamba go better in a supplement?

Appendix D - Questions

• We've just asked kids over two hundred questions like those you might ask yours. Here they are.

Which video game?
Why do you like that one?
When did you first play it?
When did it become your favorite?
Which moment?
Like when?
I can't picture it; where were you headed exactly in the fortress?
What did you do when that happened?
If you had that same moment again what would you do differently?
If you were the video game maker what would you make happen instead?
Well what choices would you provide so that something else happened?
What does your mother hate most about that?
Why does she think so?
What do you tell her?
What would you tell her?
What doesn't she quite understand?
What would make her change her mind?
Is there anything at all worrisome about that?
Is there something really good about that?
Has that made you do anything different in the world outside of gaming?
If you had to describe that as a skill, how would you describe it?
How would you teach it?

Have you learned anything bad from video games?
Would there have been a way for you to learn that outside of that game?
How did you end up scaling the wall at scout camp?
Why were you so committed to building the Tesla coil?
Why did it take so long?
Has your ACL tear changed the way you play soccer?
What specific Lego construction makes you most proud?
What do your parents argue about most?
What one thing in your backpack would you keep if it were on fire?
How much does your backpack actually weigh?
Where did you learn to meditate?
When was the moment you realized that the Legos were working?
What's one thing you have memorized by heart?
When, how, and why?
What's the most important day of your life?
Past or future?
What's the most embarrassing moment of your life so far?
When was the time you most changed your mind about something?
What moment from history would you most like to live in?
What historical person would you most like to meet?
What is the single most important thing you ever learned in school?
What is the thing you've learned that surprised you most?
If school were all one subject, which would you want it to be?
Do you have a favorite book and why?
Do you have a favorite movie and why?
Tell one great lie about yourself that you wish were true?
Tell one great truth about yourself that you wish were a lie?
How would your best friend write your epitaph?
How would your worst enemy write your epitaph?
How would you write your epitaph?
Have you ever been punched or punched someone or wished you had?
What is your essential contradiction?
What is your least popular opinion?
What opinion of yours is the one shared by the fewest other people?
What is something that you think is true that you can't prove?
What is something everyone thinks is true that you're pretty sure is false?
Which page from your autobiography would you read aloud?

I don't understand- what were you doing and why was it so expensive?
What's so special for you specifically about passive income?
How long into this project did you see the first bill?
Did you ever make as much money as quickly as you wanted?
How does ignoring requests for payment make you feel now?
Did you think $10,000 a "hilariously large number" then or now?
How did this make you feel?
That seems how you felt about being let off the hook, not getting caught.
Is that something you're glad about now or felt glad about at the time?
Why?
Again, why?
And how does that make you feel?
I wonder what great stuff she remembers that I've forgotten?
I wonder what she considers the best and worst things about herself?
I wonder what she'll discover she can do?
I wonder what she actually means by that?
I wonder what I have failed to understand about my kid?
I wonder how my kid seems to himself?
Is math a feature of the universe we discovered?
Is math a feature of the human mind at work on the universe?
Is math a system of verifiable facts or circular rules?
Is math cold truth or elegant fiction?
When was the first time you thought you might really like math?
When was the first time you encountered a truly hard math problem?
When was the most fun you've ever had with math?
"You seem to be really good at math, but do you actually love it?"
When you got the highest score on that test—what was it testing?
What was the hardest question on the test?
Was there a question you thought you got wrong but got right?
Was there a question you thought you got right but got wrong?
Is there a kind of problem in math you do differently than others do it?
Does the study of math make the world look different to you?
Do you do something other than math differently because of math?
What aspect of math makes the least sense to you?
Who is your favorite mathematician in the history of math?
What mathematical concept would you be most excited to teach me?
What do you change first about how math is taught if you're in charge?

To follow up, why?
When was that most true?
How does that feel?
Is it possible to generate a random number?
Do you have any idea what surreal numbers are?
Does math work without zero?
I don't use math at all in my job or life—or do I?
Should I?
Which exaggerated expression depicting which emotion?
Can you describe the photos you took of yourself?
Which one do you like best?
Can you tell us where, when, and which photo took hold of you?
Instead of that you think about x, can you tell what you think about x?
When did you first think about a stock photo long after you saw it?
Why
What was the actual feeling when you started looking at stock photos?
Were the feelings about the people, yourself, or something else?
Did the feelings change once you put yourself in them?
Given global extinction, how important is it that I am who I am?
Why do you love Elgar?
Which piece of music?
Which composer was your favorite before you knew Elgar?
Which piece of music?
What is this thing we know but can't prove about quadrilaterals?
Which is your favorite quadrilateral?
Which quadrilateral illustrates the failure to prove the theorem?
What one thing did your grandmother hope most for you?
What one thing did your grandmother fear most on your behalf?
What one thing will you never understand about your grandmother?
What moment during your time with this club made you most angry?
What one person joined the club because of your leadership?
Which competition will you always remember and why?
What idea from your sessions do you think changed the club most?
How did you know your club's Constitution was any good?
Why is inclusivity a priority for you as vice-president?
Is inclusion really more important than talent?
Why is cyber security so important—isn't CS all about open source?

Why is hoarding info so bad—isn't info what security keeps private?
Why include less talented people if you want to win?
Why is it so important for cricketers in Chennai to learn basketball?
Aren't you swapping a sport of empire for another from another empire?
But I thought you said x?
How could that be?
What does this have to do with that?
Could you make the opposite case?
What do you like most about coding?
Which is your favorite coding language?
If you had to spend all day coding in Java or Python which would it be?
What's an example of a variable?
And Python and Java deal differently with these things?
Flow?
Compile?
Array?
Does our own spoken language suffer the glitches of coding languages?
Like when?
How does it happen that you live with your grandma from Taiwan?
But what about programming?
But, still, does this help you program?
Well, why not walk the whole waterline then until you find the leak?
Can you stand in the gate on your horse and don't let anything by?
Will you put that uterus back in the heifer until we sew her up?
You write what you think and maybe I'll write what I think, too.
What do you think?
Why did that happen?
You mean I can just write that?
But isn't that what you just wrote?
That I'm the same as my sister?
Write this and keep writing: "The thing most similar about my sister and me is…"?
And I have a sister, too, so I'll write down the same thing and then keep writing?
How about this one: "The biggest difference between my sister and me is…"?
Should we find out what we think about our sisters?

What did your sister do that made you most mad?
What did you do that made your sister most mad?
What about your sister do you most admire?
What about you does your sister most admire?
What will you do differently next year when your sister goes off to college?
How has a generation come to think of writing as an elaborate trick?
What's the coolest thing you've ever built?
When was the very first time you ever saw a Pontiac Fiero?
How did you know you loved it?
At first you were reluctant to write that. Is it because you disagree?
Does that sound like your son?
Would you please explain what you are saying?
Can you write that down?
What do you like most about the viol da gamba?
What's your favorite piece of music to play on it?
Why?
But isn't that what you just said?

Acknowledgements

Thank you to my many students for your faith in this process, for finding and sharing what matters, and for giving me permission to borrow from our conversations.

Thank you to the many parents of these students for your insight, patience, and willingness to keep your kid in the driver's seat.

Thank you to my wife Courtney for allowing me the time and space to work on this book.

Thank you to my sister Jennifer for editing this book.

About the Author

John Dewis

John's *Hack the College Essay* is the #1 resource on Reddit's college prep forum (r/ApplyingToCollege) and a celebrated industry classic. He has helped thousands of students over two decades get into their first-choice colleges, including all the Ivies.

John is a graduate of Harvard University and Deep Springs College and has his Master's in philosophy from Claremont Graduate University.

John lives in South Pasadena with his wife and their two boys and is the incoming Head of University Lake School in Hartland, Wisconsin.

Made in United States
North Haven, CT
31 May 2023

37212045R00085